Unexplored Conditions of Charter School Principals

Other Books by
Marytza A. Gawlik and Dana L. Bickmore

The Charter School Principal: Nuanced Descriptions of Leadership

Unexplored Conditions of Charter School Principals

An Examination of the Issues and Challenges for Leaders

Edited by
Marytza A. Gawlik
Dana L. Bickmore

ROWMAN & LITTLEFIELD
Lanham • Boulder • New York • London

Published by Rowman & Littlefield
A wholly owned subsidiary of The Rowman & Littlefield Publishing Group, Inc.
4501 Forbes Boulevard, Suite 200, Lanham, Maryland 20706
www.rowman.com

Unit A, Whitacre Mews, 26-34 Stannary Street, London SE11 4AB

Copyright © 2017 by Marytza A. Gawlik and Dana L. Bickmore

All rights reserved. No part of this book may be reproduced in any form or by any electronic or mechanical means, including information storage and retrieval systems, without written permission from the publisher, except by a reviewer who may quote passages in a review.

British Library Cataloguing in Publication Information Available

Library of Congress Cataloging-in-Publication Data

Names: Gawlik, Marytza, 1973– editor. | Bickmore, Dana, 1955– editor.
Title: Unexplored conditions of charter school principals : an examination of the issues and challenges for leaders / edited by Marytza A. Gawlik and Dana L. Bickmore.
Description: Lanham : Rowman & Littlfield, [2017] | Includes bibliographical references and index.
Identifiers: LCCN 2017023101 (print) | LCCN 2017033054 (ebook) | ISBN 9781475838695 (electronic) | ISBN 9781475838671 (hardback : alk. paper) | ISBN 9781475838688 (pbk. : alk. paper)
Subjects: LCSH: Charter schools—United States—Administration. | School principals—United States.
Classification: LCC LB2806.36 (ebook) | LCC LB2806.36 .U527 2017 (print) | DDC 371.010973—dc23
LC record available at https://lccn.loc.gov/2017023101

Printed in the United States of America

Contents

Foreword   vii
   Nina K. Buchanan and Robert A. Fox

Preface   xi
   Marytza A. Gawlik and Dana L. Bickmore

Acknowledgments   xv

Introduction: Exploring Issues and Challenges   xvii
   Marytza A. Gawlik and Dana L. Bickmore

1 Charter School Principals' Autonomy in the Context of State Accountability   1
   Madeline Mavrogordato, Ellen Goldring, and Claire Smrekar

2 Charter School Leaders as Policy Actors   23
   Romina Madrid Miranda and Abigail Felber-Smith

3 How Charter School Principals Use Teacher Evaluation Systems   41
   David B. Reid

4 Balancing Progressive Education and Performance Management   61
   Erin Coghlan and Heinrich Mintrop

5 Principalship Succession and Socialization in Charter Schools   81
   Marytza A. Gawlik

Conclusion: New Looks at Charter Principal Leadership   103
   Dana L. Bickmore and Marytza A. Gawlik

Appendix A: Relevant Excerpts from the Principal Interview Protocol   111

Appendix B: Analytic Approach   113

References	115
Index	125
About the Editors	129

Foreword

Nina K. Buchanan and Robert A. Fox

The charter school movement was conceptualized as an opportunity for a local community and educators to come together and create more innovative schools designed to meet the needs of the local population. Inherent in the concept was that schools could be more effective if the staff played a greater role in setting pedagogy and instructional policy than has traditionally been the case. Schools would be largely run by teachers, under the supervision of their peers and in cooperation with parents. However, 25 years later, the charter school movement has morphed into something that would have been unrecognizable by its original proponents.

With the enthusiastic support of the federal government (seeking to "scale up" what it considers to be successful charters), multiple-campus, not-for-profit charter management organizations (CMOs) and for-profit educational management organizations (EMOs) have sprung into existence. The book refers to both types of organizations as charter school *networks*. These networks often operate from a central headquarters, and exhibit to teachers and leaders of individual schools many of the characteristics previously associated with traditional school districts.

In exchanging the pressures from "district central" for those of "network central," many on-site school leaders encounter pressures that they might not have expected when they entered the charter school universe. In this edited volume by Gawlik and Bickmore, the reader will become acquainted with the complexities of these pressures on campus leaders, whether they are called principal, director, lead teacher, or chief academic officer.

The authors of each chapter have chosen qualitative methods to illuminate specific aspects of leadership: autonomy, teacher evaluation and development, succession, and socialization. The original charter school concept of trading independence for accountability becomes blurred in the world of charter school networks. Although the scale of charter school networks has grown to span states, regions, or even the entire nation, each of the chapters in the book seeks to analyze the experiences of relatively small numbers of charter school principals in relative proximity to each other.

Indeed, the increasingly complex typology of charter schools renders it difficult to conduct large quantitative studies that treat all charter school as if they were alike. The book speaks both to educators interested in pursuing a leadership role in a charter school, and to researchers who can build on the findings presented. Perhaps the most valuable contribution of this book is to raise questions about the extent to which charter school leaders should resist forces that pull them back into the old comfortable understanding of a traditional public school principal.

Indications are that charter schools are here to stay in their many guises. We speak from our experience helping to develop the West Hawaii Explorations Academy public charter school. The agreement we and our colleagues made with the Hawaii State Department of Education, the authorizer, when we sought in 1999 to create a high school in the Natural Energy Laboratory of Hawaii was to trade autonomy for accountability to *all* state tests as well as health and safety regulations. We were even required to recognize the three labor unions representing principals, teachers, and janitors, respectively. As the number of charter schools grew, new regulations appeared, which tend to reduce autonomy.

The first chapter in this volume by Mavrogordato, Goldring, and Smrekar carefully examines the tension between autonomy and accountability as they relate to four charter schools (two stand-alone and two networked) in one urban school district in the Midwest. Unsurprisingly, they found that the school leaders were challenged by the need to remain true to the mission of the school while dealing with curriculum and making human resource and budget decisions, and at the same time pleasing the governing board, and remaining within budget limits and state testing requirements. We are left wondering whether these leaders were able to forge new paths, or ended up becoming more like the traditional system they left.

Often, neither charter school board members nor administrators realize that they need to add financial, political, and policy skill to their education portfolios. In chapter 2, Miranda and Felber-Smith explore one such intersection of charter schools and the implementation of the Minnesota Quality Compensation Policy (Q-Comp), which provided support to schools and districts to create alternative teacher compensation and professional development systems. Schools participating in Q-Comp are required to submit a plan that included performance-based pay, alternative teacher salary structures, on-the-job professional development, teacher evaluations, and opportunities for teachers to explore other careers opportunities. Q-Comp represented extra resources that would enable the schools to pay teachers more and help them improve.

However, it did not always lead to the maintenance of a cohesive school improvement plan aligned with the school's mission. Participation also came at the cost of higher external scrutiny and report keeping. Charter schools will no doubt recognize the difficulty of finding funding sources that match school goals and don't have the effect of pounding a square program into a round hole.

The findings reported in chapter 3 by Reid and in chapter 4 by Coghlan and Mintrop resonate with our experiences in Hawaii. Using performance evaluation systems with processes and forms designed for traditional classrooms won't always be the best measures of teacher performance that is meant to be organic, constructivist, and/or not classroom based. Systems that aren't aligned with the school's mission and aren't coherent with the overall school environment may end up discouraging teachers or pulling them back to traditional methods.

Finally, in chapter 5, Gawlik tackles an important but neglected topic, the succession and socialization of charter school leaders. In stand-alone charter schools with specialized missions and nontraditional expectations for leaders and teachers, finding the right fit is a challenge. Founders begin with a clear vision of the school, and operate from a position of power that can guide the school toward the vision.

The issue of succession often become critical when the founding leader retires, or chooses to leave the school. Because leadership change is often unplanned and arbitrary, individuals who work within a school and have been socialized through shared experiences, influenced by their peers as well as the leader, are in an ideal position to become leaders. Wise leaders provide opportunities for teachers to take leadership roles and develop their skills. This maximizes the chances that the culture of the school will remain consistent with its mission and vision.

The editors conclude that charter school principals need to possess a complex mix of knowledge, skills, and dispositions in order to enact the school mission while balancing the human resource needs, governance demands, and accountability requirements to keep the school in business. Readers are asked:

> Who should provide more formal preparation and professional development to charter principals so that they can more effectively engage in the unique leadership issues of charter schools? What structures should be implemented so that principals are supported as they transition to new positions? How can those responsible for effective charter schooling ease tensions among policy, principal autonomy, and school mission and vision?

John Quincy Adams offers excellent advice to charter school leaders, whether they are called principals, directors, or academic officers: "If your actions inspire others to dream more, learn more, do more, and become more, you are a leader."

Preface

Marytza A. Gawlik and Dana L. Bickmore

This book is the second in a two-volume series on the charter school principal. The first book in the series, *The Charter School Principal: Nuanced Descriptions of Leadership*, provides a foundational understanding of the charter school principalship through culture. This book, *Unexplored Conditions of Charter School Principals: An Examination of the Issues and Challenges for Leaders*, examines contemporary policy issues confronting charter school principals.

Drawing on autonomy, sensemaking, teacher evaluations, and succession and socialization, this book traces the development of the charter school principal within these policy contexts. Collectively, these topics form the beginnings of what we hope will be an informative and useful conversation of where the charter school principal has been and where the charter school principal is headed.

OVERVIEW OF THE VOLUME

This book represents an effort to document some of the issues and challenges confronting charter school principals. We solicited chapters from leading leadership and policy experts and thinkers in the field to examine the role of the charter school principalship in the context of policy reforms. In the introduction, Gawlik and Bickmore introduce the various issues and challenges that have confronted charter school leaders to this point. After situating the charter school leader in a policy context, the chapter moves towards highlighting specific themes introduced in the remaining chapters.

In chapter 1, Mavrogordato, Goldring, and Smrekar explore how charter school principals balance autonomy and accountability. They posit that charter schools are specifically designed to have more independence and more decentralized mechanisms of control, and are often exempt from regulations that apply to their traditional public school counterparts. These conditions are meant to provide charter schools with autonomy to approach educating students in new and innovative ways.

However, in practice, the autonomy that charter schools possess is often constrained. Chapter 1 presents the portraits of four charter school principals, each of whom work to balance autonomy and accountability while maintaining a relentless focus on their respective school's mission and goals.

Running a charter school poses unique conditions for principals, which can be framed as challenges and/or opportunities. Miranda and Felber-Smith explore how two charter school principals function as policy actors. More specifically, chapter 2 illuminates the principals' level of influence during policy implementation—influence that is perhaps unique to stand-alone charter school principals. Data from two schools were collected to better understand the ways in which principals and teachers made sense of the Minnesota Quality Compensation Policy (Q-Comp) and, more specifically, to explore the unique role principals play in mediating teachers' sensemaking.

In chapter 3, Reid collects and describes the responses and actions of charter school principals by documenting their perceptions, beliefs, attitudes, roles, and procedures for how they think about and evaluate the teachers in their building. Drawing on a sensemaking framework, this study followed two charter school principals in Michigan as they navigated the process of evaluating their teaching staffs. The goal of this chapter was to better understand how charter school principals make sense of teacher evaluations and, ultimately, what factors influence how they evaluate teachers in their building.

In chapter 4, Coghlan and Mintrop examine the implementation of the Teacher's Incentive Fund (TIF) through the eyes of charter school leaders who took on the program in 2010. This chapter asks how the school principals and instructional leaders at three charter schools in California balanced the tension between a performance management system and their progressive school culture, which was modeled on critical and constructivist pedagogy, a professional and autonomous adult learning climate, and a social justice school mission.

In the final chapter, Gawlik examines the ways in which charter schools manage principalship succession and direct the socialization of individuals as they move into principalship roles. Drawing on data from Florida charter schools, the results reveal variation among the schools with respect to preparation for principalship transitions and subsequent socialization.

This chapter provides a conceptual/analytic framework that can serve as a foundation for future research, which should (1) highlight the practices associated with using teacher leadership as a stepping stone to building-level principalship and (2) compare network-based and stand-alone charter schools with respect to principalship development.

In the book's conclusion, Bickmore and Gawlik summarize the findings related to the policy issues posed by authors. Also, highlighted in the conclusion are the themes that emerged across the five studies. Based on the authors' findings and the collective themes generated, the conclusion explores potential implications for charter school principals, charter organizations, policy makers, and researchers.

Acknowledgments

We want to express our gratitude to our fathers for their exceptional support and guidance. We also thank the contributors to this volume for their hard work and dedication to the field.

Introduction

Exploring Issues and Challenges

Marytza A. Gawlik and Dana L. Bickmore

No one could have anticipated, when charter schools first opened in the United States nearly three decades ago, that they would become an established part of the American public schooling landscape. Charter schools appeal to a broad range of political and ideological groups, including neoliberals, neoconservatives, the religious right, parents and teachers in urban areas, and the middle class (Wells, Grutzik, Carnochan, Slayton, & Vasudeva, 1999); however, each of these factions supports charter schools for a different reason (Apple, 1996, 2001).

Neoliberals view charter schools as a way to facilitate school choice and competition. Irrespective of consequences and outcomes, their belief in competition is crystallized, and choice is the focus of charter schooling. Neoconservatives and the religious right are more interested in removing government restrictions via deregulation and decentralization in order to create schools that emphasize moral values and religious teachings.

The urban faction, whose members have traditionally been plagued by underfunded and poorly performing schools, views the charter school movement as a way to create better schools for their children. Finally, the middle class sees charter school reform as a way to augment returns on its investment in public schooling (Apple, 1996, 2001). The wide-ranging appeal of charter schools in the United States has, to a certain extent, ensured their survival during party changes in government (Wells et al., 1999). We see this now with the current federal administration.

The growing popularity of charter schools across the political spectrum reflects a desire by many for substantial change in the public education system. Much has been written about charter schools by researchers, policy makers, and reformers, of which most is focused on student achievement, governance, and accountability. With the limited research on the charter school principalship, this second volume attempts to address the current issues and challenges confronting charter school leaders. This collection of chapters is characterized by qualitative case studies, as this is a relatively new field of exploration.

With the charter school movement entering its third decade, we have little cumulative knowledge about the issues and challenges confronted by charter principals. Have charter school principals succeeded in certain areas? Where have they fallen short? What factors and influences help explain the role of the charter school principal? As researchers and observers in education reform, we know firsthand the limited quantity of research on the charter principal produced over the past two decades. In this book, we offer an overview of the research surrounding the charter school principal.

Charter principal research has only presented broad strokes about issues these principals face, such how charter principals use the autonomy granted them, the importance of focusing on mission for charter leaders, and the greater volume of tasks required of charter principals. Limited or missing from the literature is research exploring more specific issues faced by charter school leaders, such as teacher evaluation, conflicts between mission and policy, and transitioning in leadership.

PRINCIPAL AUTONOMY

Charter schools have more autonomy (Bickmore & Gawlik, 2017; Gawlik, 2007, 2008, 2012) and generally face greater pressure to succeed than do traditional public schools (Cannata & Engel, 2012). Leaders of charter schools are expected to manage administrative and managerial duties—such as recruiting and hiring staff, and securing and maintaining facilities and funding—that are usually supported at the district level for traditional public schools. It is imperative that charter schools have the right leaders in place in order to address these administrative duties while still maintaining an instructional focus.

Charter school leaders' practices, challenges, and roles have been studied, although the research is limited. Some studies posit that fiscal and facility struggles and enhanced communication with the public are more central issues for charter school leaders than for leaders in traditional public schools (Cannata & Engel, 2012; Gross, 2011). In other studies, charter school leaders reported spending more of their time on student performance, staffing, and state standards, activities and concerns that echo those of traditional school leaders (Bickmore & Dowell, 2011, 2104; Gawlik, 2012). The research has provided additional information on leadership practices—for example, finding that teachers do not influence a charter school leader's instructional policies (Goff, Mavrogordato, & Goldring, 2012).

HUMAN RESOURCING

The tremendous growth in charter schools during the past two-and-a-half decades has occurred despite inconclusive evidence that they are academically superior to traditional public schools (Wohlstetter, Smith, & Farrell, 2013). What is important to understand are the organizational conditions of charter schools. One area where this has materialized is teacher turnover. Using data from the National Center for Education Statistics (NCES) 2003–2004 Schools and Staffing Survey (SASS) and the Teacher Follow-Up Survey (TFS), David Stuit and Thomas Smith (2010) document the trends in teacher turnover in charter schools. This has several implications for charter school principals and the work that they do.

Charter school teachers leave the profession and move between schools at higher rates than do teachers at traditional public schools (Stuit & Smith, 2010). The likelihood of a charter school teacher leaving the profession versus staying in the same school is 130 percent greater than for a traditional public school teacher (Stuit & Smith, 2010). Moreover, the odds of a charter school teacher moving to another school are 76 percent greater (Stuit & Smith, 2010).

Another important finding is that charter schools that are start-ups experience significantly more attrition and mobility than those formed by converting traditional public schools. Teachers at start-up charter schools were almost twice as likely to leave the profession and three times as likely to switch schools than teachers at conversion charters. This outcome aligns with Buddin and Zimmer's (2005) conclusion that conversion charter schools behave more like traditional public schools.

So what explains these differences? Teacher characteristics explain a large portion of the gap in turnover rates between charter school and traditional teachers. Charter school teachers are on average younger than traditional public school teachers, making them more likely to leave the profession or change schools (Stuit & Smith, 2010). They are also less likely to have an education degree or be state certified. In addition to teacher characteristics, dissatisfaction with working conditions is an important reason why teacher mobility is significantly higher in charter schools. Teacher working conditions have implications for charter principals, as teachers' perceptions of the quality of principal leadership is a dominant factor in whether teachers stay or leave a school (Ladd, 2011).

Teacher turnover is a critical issue because it has implications for the principalship within K–12 education. High turnover will have detrimental effects on school quality and result in substantial costs to schools and districts. Moreover, the pool of candidates available to enter the charter school principalship becomes somewhat limited. The organizational disruption due to high turnover among teachers makes it more difficult for charter schools to develop and sustain high levels of quality instruction over the long run.

Coupled with high teacher turnover rates in charter schools is teacher evaluation. The teacher evaluation landscape is changing in the wake of efforts to connect performance ratings and job retention to multiple measures, including the level of student learning. For those leading charter schools, the efforts are important. Charter school principals typically are not part of a central district office, and cannot rely on the support supplied to traditional public school principals. Hence, charter school principals are left to their own devices when designing and implementing a teacher evaluation system.

We know charter school teachers garner more autonomy (Gawlik, 2007), but since they tend to be newer teachers and have less experience than veteran teachers, they often struggle in the classroom setting. The way charter school teachers are evaluated has become a source of conflict between state legislatures and practitioners. Caught in the middle are charter school principals who are struggling to make sense of the evaluation system and, at the same time, implement a plan for their own school sites.

In this book, the authors provide a synthesis of the challenges confronted by charter school principals as they explore teacher evaluation systems and balance the tension between a statutory regulation and a commitment to the ideals of the charter school movement.

PRINCIPAL TURNOVER, SUCCESSION, AND SOCIALIZATION

Charter school principals are much more likely than traditional school principals to leave their schools. Seventy percent of charter school principals surveyed expected to leave their schools within five years, and 10 percent expected to move on to new opportunities or retire in the next year (Campbell, 2010). The growth of charter schools over the past 20 years clearly demonstrates their relevance as alternatives to traditional public schools. Turnover of current charter school principals is a growing concern (National Alliance for Public Charter Schools, 2014). Further, charter schools are particularly vulnerable when turnover occurs, because they are relatively "new" organizations and are unable to tap into a pool of qualified and readily available candidates when hiring.

Stable and experienced school leadership is essential for school performance (Leithwood, Patten, & Jantzi, 2010). A certain amount of turnover might be beneficial to schools if it results in a better principal-school match and the infusion of new practices and ideas (Ni, Sun, & Rorrer, 2014).

However, even when the successor is effective, the change is initially likely to have negative effects on student outcomes (Ni et al., 2014). In addition to the high costs of recruiting and developing principals, excessive principal turnover is often associated with institutional memory loss and inconsistencies in school goals, policy, and culture (Ni et al., 2014). In addition, frequent principal turnover often leads to decreased teacher commitment, increased teacher turnover, and potential disruptions in faculty efficacy (Goddard & Salloum, 2011).

Succession and socialization are complementary processes, during which a new principal influences the existing culture of a school and vice versa (Bengtson, Zepeda, & Parylo, 2013). Principalship succession is not a temporary concern, but rather a systematic issue in the public school system. The need for schools to strategically plan and manage the succession of principals is well documented. However, succession tends to fall low on the list of priorities for most charter schools. In this book, we trace a socialization framework by examining aspects of succession to highlight the challenges faced by seasoned, as well as newer, charter school principals.

POLICY IMPLEMENTATION

Collectively, these previous sections illuminate critical challenges facing charter schools and may explain in part why these schools do not systematically outperform traditional public school counterparts. Autonomy, human resourcing, and succession and socialization point to key contemporary policies affecting charter school principals in their daily work. Implementing these policies depends on the ability of social structures to shape individual and collective action to bring about desired goals.

Perhaps charter schools with central offices have the necessary social structure to do just this. In addition, granting charter school principals more autonomy must go hand in hand with professional development and capacity-building skills.

The purpose of this book is to explore the issues and challenges confronted by charter school principals across an array of goals and expectations set forth by the policy and the local context. By drawing on leadership and policy experts and researchers, we offer an in-depth examination of the current issues charter school principals face. Starting with autonomy, we work our way through teacher evaluation and succession and socialization, and then conclude with an opportunity to reflect on what we know and how to look forward.

Chapter One

Charter School Principals' Autonomy in the Context of State Accountability

Madeline Mavrogordato, Ellen Goldring, and Claire Smrekar

Advocates of charter schools assert that introducing the element of choice into the public school system will result in increased autonomy and flexibility that will in turn create conditions that spur innovation and positive change (e.g., Chubb & Moe, 1990; Walberg & Bast, 2003). Charter schools are specifically designed to have more independence and more decentralized mechanisms of control, and are often exempt from regulations that apply to their traditional public school counterparts (Bulkley & Wohlstetter, 2004; Gawlik, 2016).

These conditions are meant to provide charter schools with autonomy to approach educating students in new and innovative ways (Arsen, Plank, & Sykes, 1999; Wohlstetter, Wenning, & Briggs, 1995). For example, charter schools are free to develop their own instructional focus and curricula, recruit and enroll students, create their own academic calendars, and hire specific personnel who would best serve the needs of their students.

However, in practice, the autonomy charter schools possess is often constrained. Because charter schools are publicly funded, they are subject to the same accountability standards as traditional public schools (Gawlik, 2012), which may in turn reduce the ability of charter schools to innovate (Preston, Goldring, Berends, & Cannata, 2012). Charter schools are required to teach state academic standards, their students must take state assessments that measure student performance, and they have to participate in the same statewide systems of accountability.

Some argue that these requirements may serve to constrain charter schools' autonomy and ability to innovate; if charter schools are required to produce specific learning outcomes, they will likely coalesce around the same curricula, pedagogy, and subject areas as the traditional public schools that surround them (Barghaus & Boe, 2011; Berends, 2015; Berends, Goldring, Stein, & Cravens, 2010; Finnigan, 2007; Lubienski, 2006; Oberfield, 2016).

This inherent tension between the autonomy afforded to charter schools and the accountability requirements they must adhere to directly influences the role of the school principal. Principals are uniquely positioned to balance their school's internal priorities, values, and goals with external demands and pressures, a task that may prove more uniquely challenging in charter schools. There is limited research about how principals in charter schools balance autonomy with accountability demands. To begin to explore how charter school principals balance autonomy and accountability, this chapter will address the following questions:

1. To what extent are charter school principals afforded autonomy in their roles as leaders in their schools? What barriers do charter school principals face in capitalizing on the autonomy they are afforded?
2. How do charter school principals balance autonomy with state accountability demands? Are there differences as to how principals balance autonomy and accountability across independent charter schools and those affiliated with a broader network of schools?

BACKGROUND

In theory, charter schools should alter the traditional roles of all stakeholders involved in the education of children, including principals (Chubb & Moe, 1990; Hausman & Goldring, 2001). Charter schools are assumed to be associated with bottom-up reform that is characterized by increased autonomy and reduced bureaucracy, both of which are meant to empower charter school educators, including school leaders (Miron & Nelson, 2002). Changes in principals' roles are predicted to stem not only from an increase in autonomy, but also the need for charter school principals to attend to a host of responsibilities not associated with traditional school leadership.

Indeed, data from a survey of charter school leaders shows that principals face new and different challenges, including recruiting students, fundraising, managing facilities, and negotiating with the traditional public school districts in which they are located, none of which are a concern for traditional public school principals (Campbell & Grubb, 2008). While the literature suggests that school organizational conditions and leadership practices may be configured differently under school choice reforms, there is very little empirical research that examines principals in charter schools. We discuss this limited extant research below.

Principal Autonomy

With the movement toward increased accountability for student performance, there have been simultaneous calls for principals to have more autonomy for improving teaching and learning in their schools (Louis, Leithwood, Wahlstrom, & Anderson, 2010; Robinson, Lloyd, & Rowe, 2008). Principal autonomy is at the core of the rationale behind charter schools. We define autonomy as the "independence and self-determination of a community in its external and internal relations" (Wohlstetter et al., 1995, p. 338).

Principals are generally thought to have a fair amount of professional autonomy in their work; as Gawlik (2008) describes, "When the school door closes, each principal determines the manner in which he or she will work" (p. 785). Theory suggests that charter school principals may experience heightened autonomy due to the conditions created by deregulation and decentralization (Fuller, 2000), and that this will empower them to make decisions that will lead to positive results for students and teachers. Moreover, because principals impact the professional culture of an entire school, the autonomy that charter school principals are posited to possess is a critical element in the arguments underpinning the charter school movement.

Only a few researchers have explored principal autonomy in charter schools. Triant (2001) examined eight charter school principals in Massachusetts, and found that autonomy around hiring teachers and having control over the budget was particularly important, but that principals were often constrained by a need to cut costs. Portin, Schneider, DeArmond, and Gundlach (2003) found that principals in charter and magnet schools tend to have more authority and distribute more of their leadership than do peers who lead traditional public schools.

A study of successful charter schools found that principal autonomy is focused in the following areas: developing a team, managing teachers, curriculum and classroom structures, scheduling, finances, and defining a unique school culture (Ableidinger & Hassel, 2010). The principals in these schools asserted that their autonomy is critical to their work, allowing them to make decisions and act in ways that have led to high student performance (Ableidinger & Hassel, 2010).

In one of the only quantitative studies of principal autonomy, Gawlik (2008) used national data to examine principals' perceived influence on several domains. She found that principals in start-up charter schools perceive greater influence than their peers in traditional public schools and those in conversion charter schools (preexisting public and private schools that had converted to charter schools), particularly exerting more influence over performance standards, curriculum, professional development programming, hiring and evaluating teachers, discipline policy, and budget decisions. Gawlik (2008) asserts that this may be because principals in start-up charter schools "are not burdened with institutional history . . . and may reflect greater autonomy from external (bureaucratic) control" (p. 796).

As demonstrated by Gawlik's (2008) findings, there is evidence that the autonomy afforded to principals may vary within the charter school sector. While Gawlik (2008) investigated differences in principal autonomy between newly founded start-up charter schools and older traditional public and private schools that had converted to charter schools, this study did not examine whether principals at independent charter schools experience different levels of autonomy than their peers at charter schools affiliated with a broader network of schools, such as a charter management organization (CMO).

These broader networks of schools are seen as models that may allow for effective charter schools to scale up more rapidly and create economies of scale by drawing from common central-office resources and expertise (Farrell, Wohlstetter & Smith, 2012). While a networked system may offer many advantages, it is possible that charter schools that are part of these systems do not possess as much autonomy, because they must ascribe to a particular model or mission (Lake, Dusseault, Bowen, Demeritt, & Hill, 2010). In essence, networked charter schools may experience greater levels of bureaucracy, the very thing charter schools were meant to avoid in the first place.

Research investigating the autonomy of principals across independent and networked charter schools is scant. Cravens, Goldring, and Peñaloza (2009) found that principals in schools affiliated with CMOs do spend their time in different ways. For example, CMO principals spend less time promoting the school to parents and obtaining school facilities compared with principals at independent charter schools, suggesting that these differences in leadership practices may be due to the unique organizational features and governance structures of these schools. Yet it remains unclear whether principals in these different types of charter schools are afforded differing amounts of autonomy.

This chapter seeks to build on the limited prior work on principal autonomy in charter schools, by investigating how principals reconcile accountability demands with their autonomy in independent and affiliated charter schools.

DATA AND METHODS

Our study examines how principals' leadership roles reflect autonomy across charter schools that are located within one Midwestern urban school district and overseen by the same charter authorizer. We purposefully selected four case study charter schools. We sought to include a broad spectrum of schools in the study in an effort to capture variability in the roles principals may play in the charter school context. For example, we sought to include schools that were independently operated and those that were affiliated with a broader network of schools, because we hypothesize that these different governance structures may shape the extent to which principals are afforded autonomy in their work. Our sample included the following schools:[1]

1. King College Preparatory Academy: An independent school with a history of meeting adequate yearly progress (AYP), serving nearly 100 percent African American students in grades 6–12; the school continues to be led by the founding principal.
2. Davis Community Charter School: A small independent school located in a historic African American neighborhood with close ties to a community nonprofit organization; the school serves students in grades K–6, and is undergoing a period of transition between the founding and incoming administrators.
3. Gatlin School: A school with a history of academic success; one of a network of five international schools opened by the same founder that serves a diverse student body.
4. Star Academy: A school managed by a large national CMO, serving students in grades pre-K through 8, that has yet to meet AYP.

Each on-site case study included semi-structured interviews with administrators, faculty, and staff across three to five days. More than 20 interviews were conducted at each school. Researchers collected documents and other artifacts, observed teachers and leaders throughout their visit, and kept detailed observation notes. Interview questions focused around such themes as governance and accountability, teaching and learning environment, and teacher recruitment, retention, and evaluation. Relevant excerpts from the interview protocol are included in appendix A.

Given this chapter's focus on how charter school principals balance autonomy with accountability demands, we rely primarily on school principal interviews and observation data. Information on each principal can be found in table 1.1. Details on how data were analyzed can be found in Appendix B.

FINDINGS

Charter School Principals' Autonomy

The charter school principals all indicated that they possess varying degrees of autonomy, and that they view autonomy as an important condition of their

Table 1.1. Case Study Schools and Principals

School	Independent/ CMO	Mission Overview	Principal	Background Information on Principal
Davis Community Charter School	Independent	Educate the whole child and promote life-long learning	Ms. Jones	Ms. Jones has been principal of this school for decades; oversaw conversion from a private school to a charter school in the mid-2000s.
Gatlin School	Affiliated with international network of schools	Promote life-long learning, character development, and prepare students to contribute to society	Ms. Smith	Ms. Smith has been principal of this school for the past three years; previously she served as a principal at a local traditional public school for six years.
King College Preparatory Academy	Independent	Prepare students for college regardless of their past academic preparation	Mr. West	Mr. West was recruited by the charter school's board to serve as the school's founding principal; had experience teaching in private school settings and in college admissions, but no prior experience in educational administration.

School	Independent/ CMO	Mission Overview	Principal	Background Information on Principal
Star Academy	CMO with schools in five states	Provide students with rigorous academic coursework as well as fine and performing arts curriculum	Ms. Ryan	Ms. Ryan has been principal for one year; she had worked in traditional public schools for the prior 16 years as a teacher, assistant principal, and principal.

work. Perspectives on autonomy were to some extent shaped by the principals' prior school leadership experiences. Principals at Gatlin School and Star Academy had previously worked as principals in a traditional public school setting, and both agreed that they had much more autonomy in a charter school setting. Ms. Smith explained the difference clearly:

> The chief difference is that in [the traditional public school district], I had pretty limited control. I had an endless list of policies, procedures, contractual agreements, and things like that that I had to abide by, so doing anything innovative or trying to create change was a huge task. Here, we are a nonunion school, so there is no master contract. My school board is appointed, not elected. So everybody that sits on the board is of like mind and wants the school to do well. And we find that if we are sitting on teachers that either don't have the skills or capabilities, that don't have the right attitude, we can make a change.

Conversely, principals at Davis Community Charter School and King College Preparatory Academy had previously worked in private school settings, and both indicated that they were hesitant to take positions in charter schools because of the autonomy they would have to relinquish. Ms. Jones recalled her concern about losing control over student admissions: "Needless to say, I did not want to go for charter because it meant you had to accept everyone. I said, oh, I don't know how this is going to work. That means we have to take everybody."

Across the schools in our study, principals noted the importance of autonomy in four areas: (1) enacting the school's mission, (2) academic model/ curriculum, (3) human resources, and (4) budgeting. Areas of autonomy are summarized in table 1.2.

Enacting the School's Mission

Proponents of school choice assert that charter schools are better positioned to adopt innovative missions and have the flexibility to be more mission-driven than traditional public schools (Berends, 2015). Each school's mission

Table 1.2. Summary of Areas of Autonomy and Autonomy Constraints

Areas in Which Charter School Principals Possess Autonomy	
Enacting the school's mission	• Principals make the school's educational approach, mission, and values clear to stakeholders, including school staff, parents, and community members. • Principals are heavily invested in keeping the mission of the school at the forefront of practice.
Academic model/curriculum	• Principals have the freedom to make changes so long as these changes were in line with the school's underlying mission and values. • Principals have discretion to allocate funding to purchase curricular materials and to offer professional development to teachers.
Human resources	• Principals possess autonomy over who they hired and who they released. • Principals are able to dismiss teachers who are not performing or are not a good fit for their school.
Budgeting	• Principals can allocate funding to pay for initiatives that they believe are important for enacting their school's mission. • Principals have the autonomy to voluntarily partner with external funders to obtain the necessary resources to accomplish their goals.
Autonomy Constraints	
Budget constraints	• Principals are limited from capitalizing on their autonomy because of tight budgets, at times due to charter schools receiving less funding than traditional public schools. • Principals must make trade-offs due to budget limitations.
Capacity constraints	• Principals do not have the capacity in their schools to capitalize on their autonomy. • Principals struggle to implement innovative practices due to inexperienced or overwhelmed staff.
Misalignment with the board's priorities	• Principals have to put aside some of their priorities in favor of carrying out what board members prefer. • Principals are required to balance the priorities they have for their schools with those of board members.

was central to the work principals do; each case study school had a particular mission to guide their school's unique approach to educating children.

The principal's role was to make the school's educational approach, mission, and values clear to stakeholders, including school staff, parents, and community members. Although three out of four principals were hired after the school mission had been determined, typically by the school board or CMO, principals were heavily invested in keeping the mission of the school at the forefront of practice. Ms. Smith, principal at Gatlin School, indicated that she is "the person that communicates the mission, that tells the story. I very much see myself as the keeper of the vision."

All principals indicated that they had autonomy over how they went about enacting the mission. As Mr. West explained:

> What I found fascinating about [King College Prep] was the notion that a high school would push kids universally toward selective college admission. Of course, I had to define what that meant. . . . And so the only given here is the mission: That every kid will qualify for selective college admission upon graduation. The other stuff, we'll change it as we need to change it.

In line with previous research (e.g., Wohlstetter, Malloy, Hentschke, & Smith, 2004; Wohlstetter, Malloy, Smith, & Hentschke, 2004), principals in our study also used their autonomy to reach out to and partner with external organizations and agencies that had overlapping missions. Ms. Smith explained that she targets "organizations that have a similar philosophy, wanting to help impoverished kids or at-risk kids, things like that, and approach them and say, hey, we hear that you want to work with poor kids. Guess what? We have a building full of poor kids. Let's work together." While the mission itself was non-negotiable, all principals expressed that they were afforded autonomy over how to best implement the mission on the ground.

Academic Model/Curriculum

Because charter schools are exempt from many of the rules and regulations that govern traditional public schools, theory suggests that charter schools can be more innovative (e.g., Chubb & Moe, 1990; Walberg & Bast, 2003). The hope is that this innovation will be reflected in charter schools' curricula and pedagogy, two areas that have the potential to meaningfully reshape students' learning experiences.

Principals discussed varying levels of autonomy over their school's academic model and/or curriculum. Three principals indicated that when they were dissatisfied with a curriculum, they had the freedom to investigate other options and make a change. Ms. Jones discussed how simple it was for her school to switch their curriculum: "[A curriculum company] did a pilot here for math. And we were not happy with it at all. So even though they had given the pilot and all, we changed." Similarly, Ms. Smith reported being unhappy with the curriculum when she arrived at Gatlin, and described her efforts to change it:

> When I got here, this school was using a programmed curriculum. You use the script that you read, that whole thing. My philosophy is, that is a load of crap. What we do now, stuck with the same values and the same direction, where they wanted to go, I just didn't think that was the right way to do it. So, [we now use] the Responsive Classrooms model.

A common theme is that principals generally felt that they had the freedom to make changes, so long as these changes were in line with the school's underlying mission and values. They had discretionary funding to purchase curricular materials and to offer professional development to teachers.

Human Resources

Prior research suggests that one of the areas in which charter schools differ substantially from traditional public schools is personnel policies. Charter schools are known for having more flexibility in hiring and dismissal practices, in addition to the freedom to compensate teachers in nontraditional ways (Podgursky, 2008). Much of this leeway stems from the fact that charter school teachers are much less likely to be unionized, and therefore do not participate in collective bargaining agreements.

The principals reported high levels of autonomy over who they hired and who they released. Principals talked about the importance of being able to let go of a teacher who is not performing or is not a good fit for their school. As Mr. West voiced, "I'm never concerned about the teacher who's in left field, because I have a response that's pretty effective. Find a new job." Every principal reported releasing teachers who had not been performing adequately, or were not well aligned with the mission of the school.

Charter schools often have higher rates of teacher turnover, but principals indicated that this "churn" is not necessarily a problem, but is more reflective of their autonomy in recruiting and hiring teachers who aligned with the mission. For example, Mr. West believed that it was important to bring teachers with nontraditional teaching backgrounds into his school, because of the academic content area expertise they brought to the table.

> I hired a kid, he had a biology degree from Morehouse College. And a master's in education from Harvard. But it wasn't a transition to teaching program, it was mind, brain, cognitive science kind of stuff. And so, he wanted to go to medical school. It was his dream to be a doctor. He had just finished his master's at Harvard and wanted to teach biology. Well, while he was here he strengthened our biology program. He took chemistry to a whole different level. He got us engaged with some different people in partnership. And then

he went to medical school. I'd do it all over again because the kids not only got a lot from him as a scientist and somebody who understood science at a deeper level, but they're also inspired by the fact that he went to medical school. And so that pays big dividends. They still email him, he's still connected to their lives, a whole lot. And so replacing him is difficult, right? But I think that makes a lot more sense than hiring somebody just out of school with little experience, fragmented science background. You know, you need big brains to get this done.

Principals evidently possessed autonomy over teacher compensation, which was reflected in the variation in compensation packages for teachers across schools. For example, Ms. Ryan said she has "a lot of discretion" when it comes to determining teachers' salaries at Star Academy. Principal Smith explained that she chose to compensate teachers for this additional time by offering merit pay:

> So, the way it works is . . . if you did a good job, you got your merit increase, you got your bonus, you make a little bit more here. It is not much more, but it is a little bit more. And then you have a lot of flexibility and freedom to make decisions, to spearhead projects; if something really isn't working for you and you want to change, whether you dislike the textbook that we are using or you really want to see us do an Earth Day project, whatever it might be, if it is easy for us to do and you are passionate about it, it will probably happen. Those are some of the big drivers.

Moreover, Ms. Smith explained how she had the freedom to change the way the bonus was determined when she became principal at Gatlin:

> The merit scale was already in place, but the structure, I came up with the structure. The bonus was in place, but it was totally arbitrary. . . . Now, we look at where we are at the end of the year, the school-wide target where we said we need to get to this point. So, if we get to this point, then everybody has an equal share in getting there. Because we don't give the same test throughout the whole building, the targets are a little bit different, but the way it is calculated is all the same.

Principals also had the autonomy to think creatively about how to improve teacher performance. One principal in particular, Mr. West, chose to approach this process differently by recording every classroom:

> We are now just moving to a point, though, where we're going to start using [classroom video recording] to move the instructional program. We just had the software migrate to one of the classrooms that has a projector mounted to the ceiling. And so the next phase of moving instructional culture will be to say, hey, let's watch it and let's evaluate. Everybody, use the classroom observation rubric that we use when we come in the classroom, and you tell us what you see.

Unlike Mr. West, most principals reported using teacher performance monitoring strategies that paralleled what is commonplace in traditional public schools, including classroom observations, walk-throughs, and rubrics. However, as is evidenced by Mr. West's use of video cameras, principals had the autonomy to think differently about monitoring teacher performance.

Budgeting

Principals felt that they possessed substantial control over their school's finances. Ms. Ryan explained:

> With regard to my budget, I feel like I am experiencing the autonomy to do what I need to do for my particular school. The only person that I have to justify why I'm doing things is my local board, and that is with their feedback and under the advisement of my regional director. I don't feel the pressure to put things in that I don't need, or abandon programs or things that aren't useful to me.

Moreover, the principals explained that they can divert funding to pay for initiatives that they believe are important to enacting the school's mission. Ms. Smith recalled moving some funding to help encourage teachers to do home visits:

> We put a financial incentive out there where teachers got paid for going on these home visits. The staff that went, the early adopters, were pretty enthusiastic about it, so I had them speak and kind of give their testimony at the staff meeting about how they were impressed, how they were shocked, how they couldn't believe whatever it was. They had to turn in this sheet to get paid, and they had to tell me what their experience was.

Some principals also had the autonomy to voluntarily partner with external funders to obtain the necessary resources to accomplish their goals. Mr. West reported reaching out to the Gates Foundation to seek an implementation grant to fund their early college partnership with a local institution of higher education:

> The $320,000 from the Gates Foundation helped us to essentially establish our early college program. It funded that work, it funded curriculum development to make sure that we were developing a program underneath early college that would truly feed it, so that we wouldn't wind up with a group of kids who did qualify and a group of kids who didn't. And it funded some teacher development and orientation to train them to do this work.

In two charter schools, Gatlin and Davis, partnering with private foundations was more obligatory due to arrangements with the charter school founder or affiliations with local organizations. Ms. Smith reported receiving funding from the private foundation that supported the broader international network of schools, but explained that she had little autonomy when it came to deciding how to use that money:

> We get a yearly pledge of support from [the founder's organization] and over the year we draw that money down. And we are accountable to report back on how we spend that money. So that is the official relationship. The reality is that they are the landlord. They own the buildings. We have to pay them rent, where the bulk of that rent comes out of the yearly support that they give us. It is one of those types of arrangements . . . 12 percent of our budget comes from [them]. So it is a very significant piece of our budget.

Despite the fact that some principals had to contend with the priorities of their founders or those of affiliated organizations, principals agreed that they possessed much more control over their budget relative to their peers in traditional public schools. Ms. Smith, a principal who had previously served as an administrator in a traditional public school, made it clear that she believed she possessed much more discretion over how to spend money at her school:

> One of the things that I think is really important that I didn't have control over in [the traditional public school] was the leader of the school having complete control over the entire budget. I had control over at best, maybe 1/16th of my total budget at [the public school]. There is very little money that I could actually direct toward certain things. Here, I have complete control over the budgeting, the expenditures. I have to approve every single expenditure and sign every check, which is a system that I set up to ensure the integrity of that, because I think it is so important. So if there is something that is really, really important that I know will make a difference, I reallocate money and make a decision about what is the least important thing we have that I can divert money from. It is a constant balancing act to try and ensure that we put the funds where we are going to get the most results.

Overall, principals expressed substantial leeway regarding their budgets and ability to determine their own financial priorities, and they agreed that this financial autonomy was an important condition of being able to accomplish their goals as charter school principals.

Conditions Inhibiting Charter School Principals from Capitalizing on Autonomy

While principals all believe they possess autonomy that allows them to approach school leadership differently than leaders in traditional public schools, there are also conditions that constrain their ability to capitalize on their autonomy. Discussions with principals suggest three reasons that limit principals' autonomy: (1) budget constraints, (2) limited capacity, and (3) misalignment with their school board's priorities. Autonomy constraints are summarized in table 1.2.

Budget Constraints

While budget constraints are arguably a limitation for principals across all schools, they may be particularly pronounced for charter school principals since charter schools tend to receive less funding than traditional public schools (Speakman, 2008). Principals reported that they did not receive funding for facilities, nor did they receive funding to provide transportation for students.[2] Consequently, they had to divert funding to pay for their school buildings and make tough decisions about providing busing for students. Ms. Jones discussed the hefty amount her school pays to supplement their existing facility with portable classrooms:

> We pay rent. That is $6,500 a month for each one of these modulars, or the learning cottages as we call them, because we don't want kids to say they are in the modulars, they are in the trailers, no, you are in the learning cottage. Then you have to pay for the ramp, then you pay for the little porch areas, all of that is separate. So we are paying about $10,000 a month for these. That is about $120,000 a year, because you pay for them in the summer.

Mr. West explained that they offer to pay for city bus passes at King College Prep, but they cannot afford to bus students since they draw students from all over the city. Principal Ryan explained that her school loses students through the year because they are not able to accommodate new bus stops when families move: "We lost a lot, transportation kills us because we have satellite stops. I don't know if parents don't understand that I can't get them a bus stop, or they are just not accepting of it. So if they have to move, they can't come back. And that is disheartening, that is frustrating."

Because money gets diverted to pay for facilities and transportation, principals explain that there must be trade-offs elsewhere in the budget. Mr. West discusses how these budget constraints prompted him to forgo an attractive academic model in favor of adopting one for which they could strike a financial deal:

> We looked at the International Baccalaureate program, which we loved, but when we considered the expense of doing IB, there was just no way we could fund an all IB program. Well, we struck a deal because we were a start-up. One of our teachers, Ms. Smart, would consent to be on National Faculty for Accelerated Schools, and the $45,000 annual fee to be part of Accelerated Schools would be waived. But the deal is that Accelerated Schools could call anytime and ask Ms. Smart to do anything. Honestly, if they called and said, "we need Ms. Smart in New Orleans for a week," she would have to go.

Similarly, principals report having to make some tough decisions regarding teaching staff, due to budget constraints. At times, principals were unable to afford the teachers they would have liked to hire. As Ms. Ryan explained, "We are finally getting music, and I had a fabulous candidate who came to me, highly recommended, and [a local public school] offered her a position and I couldn't match it because in doing that I wouldn't be able to spread the salaries out for Spanish and PE and art. So I had to let her go, I couldn't offer her the same."

Charter school principals evidently experience greater autonomy over their budget, but they face a number of real and substantial budget constraints that at times make it difficult to make use of their autonomy.

Capacity Constraints

One of the reasons charter schools have proliferated is the belief that, because they possess organizational independence and freedom from many of the regulations that govern traditional public schools, they are better positioned to try new and innovative approaches to education (Lubienski, 2003, 2004). However, charter schools do not necessarily have the capacity, in terms of personnel, expertise, or other resources, to realize meaningful changes in education (Preston et al., 2012).

Unlike traditional public schools, charter schools, particularly those that are not affiliated with a larger network or management organization, do not generally have access to district-level administrative support (Farrell, Nayfack, Smith, & Wohlstetter, 2014). For example, traditional public schools often receive support, training, and resources from district personnel to serve students with special educational needs and English learners, and have district staff who provide assistance with curriculum and instruction. Not having access to these district-level supports may mean that charter schools do not possess the capacity to implement innovative practices.

A common theme among principals is that they do not have the capacity to capitalize on the autonomy they possess to make meaningful educational changes. Mr. West discussed an attempt to develop a curriculum from scratch when King College Prep first opened, and butting up against capacity constraints, particularly since the teaching staff had such limited experience:

> We took two months constructing a school. Basically saying, okay, here are the non-negotiables. These are the course titles, here are the state standards. Well, we didn't have a team strong enough to do that. You need people who are already secure in their instructional practice. They're already kind of dyed in the wool about instructional organization and classroom management. They didn't have the content-level expertise to dig into the content, figure out ways of knowing and uncovering knowledge. Basically, we overwhelmed them and we wound up with curriculum products that were indefensible. So, we had to

kind of back up, and then go at curriculum development from a different way, driving it from the front office.

Ms. Smith also discussed her plans to use a curricular model instead of having teachers generate the curriculum due to a lack of capacity:

> The goal of the school was to start off with this very defined, structured, but hands-on, teacher-driven curriculum. We are not there yet. We do a great job in the lower grades, pretty good in the intermediate, and then it falls apart at the middle school level. The hang-up we have right now is that I don't personally have the capacity to develop a whole new instructional model based on project-based learning. I personally had done lots of schematic teaching when I was a teacher. So we are looking at Expeditionary Learning as our model at the middle school.

These examples display a similar pattern. First, principals set out to create something new and innovative. Then they realize their school lacks the capacity to do so effectively. Finally, they compromise by defaulting, at least in part, to a readily available curriculum, or prevailing practice, and try to integrate more innovative practices gradually over time as they build their staff's capacity. Given the higher rates of teacher turnover in charter schools, this raises important questions about whether principals in these schools can build the necessary capacity to innovate and capitalize on their autonomy.

Misalignment with the Board's Priorities

Charter schools are overseen by a board of trustees, which helps govern the school and fulfills fiduciary obligations (Goldring & Mavrogordato, 2011). Charter school principals are hired by and report to this board. Because of the authority these charter school boards possess, principals may at times have to put aside some of their priorities to carry out what board members prefer (Gawlik, 2015; Ni, Sun, & Rorrer, 2014). Two principals reported disagreeing with the board sometimes, and having to revise their plans to satisfy the board. Ms. Smith recounted a time she felt compelled to follow the board even when she disagreed with board members, because it was important to maintain a positive relationship:

> That was one of the times when I decided it was better to roll forward than keep arguing, because I was going to lose that argument with [the board member] and she was passionate about single-sex classes. And so, we went ahead and gave it a shot. It created more problems than it solved. I never would have chosen to do single-sex classes. It was something that the board was really pushing for, and for me to maintain my good relationship with them, it has to be give and take. I pick and choose my battles.

Mr. West discussed his preference for additional administrators to help support students, but his board disagreed:

> We started with two more administrators than we have right now. Our board continues to feel like more money should go to the classroom, so if I say I've got to have another teacher, they go, "sure, spend that money," even if it takes us over budget, they say "doesn't matter, you've got to have another teacher." But if I say, I need another assistant principal because I need somebody else who's doing student-level interaction and support, our board says, "maybe next year. Maybe two years from now."

These examples demonstrate that some of principals' autonomy seems to be curtailed by their school boards. Principals are required to balance the priorities they have for their schools with those of board members.

Balancing Autonomy with State Accountability Demands

The charter school principals indicate that they possess notable autonomy in enacting the mission, shaping the academic model/curriculum, human resources, and budgeting. However, their autonomy is also reduced due to budget constraints, limited capacity in their schools, and a need to satisfy their board of trustees. Given that charter school principals do possess some autonomy, how do they balance this autonomy with state accountability demands?

For principals, meeting accountability standards was a clear priority, and something to be taken very seriously. Ms. Jones's commitment to meeting accountability requirements was demonstrated when she recalled her frustration with a former assistant principal who was not as concerned about student performance on the state standardized test: "I looked up and for the test, the kids had on pajamas. I almost died. Because to me, the test is serious business. And that year our scores went down. She had told the teachers that the kids could wear pajamas and just relax. I almost had a stroke."

Other principals echoed the prioritization of accountability:

> Our very first staff meeting was, this is the state standard. This is what the kids, the state is holding us accountable to, let's unpack it. What does that mean? This whole year has been a training on state standards. (Ms. Ryan, Star Academy)

> If you can produce results, I'm not going to penalize because you do it differently. As long as you can get the results, I'm not going to worry about it. Diversity is wonderful. (Ms. Smith, Gatlin School)

> I try to let the teachers have freedom. But the thing is, with their freedom, you had better believe that if I come into your classroom, you had better be teach-

ing. You still have to meet that state academic standard. (Ms. Jones, Davis Community Charter School)

While meeting accountability requirements was a priority for all four principals in our study, the principals did not necessarily think that accountability systems were inherently constraining their autonomy if the outcomes emphasized in the systems aligned well with the school's mission. For example, the mission at King was to prepare students for college. Mr. West explained, "The one non-negotiable at [King] is the outcome. And the outcome is pretty serious, because it's not just about college readiness, it's about college immersion. And so from that standpoint, that's what we do and who we are." Therefore, a laser focus on academic performance in core subject areas aligned well with the state accountability system's priorities.

At two schools, King College Prep and Gatlin, principals felt that they could use their autonomy to improve student performance. Mr. West provided an illustrative example:

> We don't want to plateau here. We want to keep moving forward. . . . To pull our kids to, say, almost 77 percent proficiency on the state exam has been like pulling teeth. And, if we keep doing what we're doing, we'll probably continue to hover in the area of three-quarters of our kids are proficient, however going to the next level will mean some retooling because there are some kids, almost a full quarter, who are not getting what they need yet. I think it's going to mean more contact time with kids and families. And I think it's going to mean a more overt kind of academic support to give kids capacity. Basically, it's just going to mean more of teachers' time. We already do nine hours, four days a week, and eight on Friday, but it's going to mean some Saturday time. It's going to have to be mandatory to work with kids who are still not getting what they need.

Mr. West's approach to increasing student performance—requiring his teachers and staff to put in more hours with students—is one that reflects his autonomy as a charter school principal. Such an approach would likely be untenable in most traditional public schools, where contracts define the amount of time teachers work.

Conversely, principals did at times report having difficulty balancing their school's mission with accountability metrics when their school was interested in outcomes that extended beyond those emphasized in their state's accountability system. For example, Ms. Ryan recalled that when she first began as principal, she was uncomfortable devoting half an hour at the beginning of each day to classroom meetings instead of academic instruction:

> Our teachers start off with their morning meetings, and Circle of Power and Respect. As an administrator coming in, I'm thinking to myself, "That is down time, you have been in school for 30 minutes, that instruction should have

started." And they are like, "Wait a minute. You have forgotten why they are even here, giving them that opportunity." I'm like, "OK, you are sharing. Share for 5 minutes and get going." But the teachers were adamant, "No, then that will lose the whole purpose of being a charter school."

Moreover, Ms. Ryan indicated it was challenging to continue to keep arts education at the center of their work at Star Academy: "But right now, the focus has been so much on engagement and rigor, we are losing the art infusion piece. So we are trying to be very intentional about making sure that piece does not get lost."

Thus, principals at times experienced a tension between autonomy and accountability if their school was interested in outcomes other than those emphasized by the state. Principals were able to use their autonomy as long as it served to improve outcomes that align with those prioritized in the state accountability system (e.g., math and reading performance). However, it was clear that the principals' freedom was curtailed by a need to focus on demonstrating proficiency on state assessments.

Balancing Autonomy and Accountability: Independent Charter Schools Compared to Affiliated Charter Schools

Two of the charter schools in our sample were affiliated with a broader network of schools. Star Academy was a member of a CMO with schools across five different states, and Gatlin School was part of an international network of schools. Having these schools in our sample allows us to explore whether there are differences in autonomy across affiliated and independent schools.

Charter schools that are affiliated with a broader network of schools such as a CMO have the potential to provide the organizational structure, capacity, and support that make it easier to lead a successful school. Principals in affiliated charter schools may not be faced with as many administrative duties, or may not need to wear as many hats as their peers in independent charter schools. Mr. West, principal of an independent charter school, noted this distinction: "Some charter schools start and are an offshoot of an existing [CMO]. They have the organizational capacity already. They could tap their CFO to provide some financial stewardship; they could get their attorney to provide some legal work."

Despite the fact that affiliating with a broader network may provide support, these may restrict principals' autonomy by requiring principals to enact specific models and strategies that are consistent with the broader network of schools. Membership could ultimately reduce autonomy and increase bureaucracy (Goldring & Mavrogordato, 2011).

Ms. Ryan's comments reflected some of the tension that existed between balancing the priorities of her school's CMO with the accountability context in her state. This tension is perhaps best exemplified in a discussion of how challenging it was for her to change her school's curriculum. Ms. Ryan recalled how she had to work to convince the CMO to make these changes: "Flipping that pancake was rough. Because we had to provide the rationale [to the CMO]." The CMO had been hesitant to allow her to deviate from the curriculum for fear of losing consistency across their network of schools, but ultimately gave in when she convinced the CMO that their curriculum was not well aligned with state standards: "We had to provide the rationale to change the curriculum, and the only way we could provide the rationale was with data. And that data is scary, because when you open up that data they are like, 'wait a minute, so we are not passing?' No. And with No Child Left Behind and Adequate Yearly Progress, the state could come in here and reconstitute."

While Ms. Ryan was ultimately able to get her CMO to allow her school to deviate somewhat from the curriculum, she described having to maintain some amount of "fidelity to the curriculum because it still provides us the consistency that we need across the network." Thus, while the principal received quite a bit of support from her CMO through their education team, tech support, and facilities management, the trade-off was less autonomy and decision-making authority as a charter school principal.

DISCUSSION

This chapter describes the domains and boundaries of principal autonomy in charter schools. Principals highlighted the importance of autonomy in enhancing their ability to lead their schools toward success. Importantly, the domains of their autonomy correspond to those roles most associated with leadership, roles that research suggests are closely aligned with raising student achievement: (1) enacting the school's mission, (2) academic model/ curriculum, (3) human resources, and (4) budgeting.

Research on effective schools reminds us that principals' engagement in key activities is most likely to reap benefits for student achievement (e.g., Harris, Rutledge, Ingle, & Thompson, 2010; Knapp, Copland, Plecki, & Portin, 2006). These activities are closely aligned with those areas where charter school principals noted they had or desired autonomy, and include:

- Principals' involvement in framing and sustaining their schools' vision or mission, and planning specific goals and strategies for school improvement aligned with the mission;
- Principals' engagement with monitoring instruction and providing feedback, analyzing student data, and supporting teachers' professional development;

- Principals' work to enhance the organizational and social structures in their schools;
- Principals' efforts to improve the culture or climate in their schools; and
- Principals' focus on personnel by hiring and retaining qualified teachers.

However, there are boundaries and constraints to charter school principal autonomy. Charter schools are not independent private schools; they are part of a public school system that faces inherent challenges. Like all schools, charter school principals wrestle with budget limitations and capacity constraints that have direct implications for their levels of autonomy. Without outside expertise and a network of supports, and sufficient resources, the charter school principals featured in this chapter were not always able to realize or implement their programmatic ideas in such areas as curriculum and program redesign.

Thus, the success of charter schools is not simply a matter of principal autonomy, but also requires leadership skills to navigate the larger constraints inherent in any school system. This might be most prevalent in those charter schools that are affiliated with a broader network, such as a CMO.

However, being affiliated with a broader network of schools also appears to provide added capacity to charter schools that may help schools manage accountability requirements. At CMOs, principals may spend less time on more administrative or managerial aspects of leadership such as managing facilities and budgeting, because these tasks are, at least in part, facilitated by central CMO staff. This may better allow principals to focus on improving the core aspects of schooling: teaching and learning.

Moreover, the CMO may provide additional resources that would otherwise be unavailable or unaffordable to charter school principals. Expertise from specialized personnel may help principals at affiliated schools better serve students with special learning needs and provide stronger professional development opportunities for their teaching staff, thereby helping improve student performance.

Accountability requirements and pressures are at the forefront of charter school principals' leadership. This is no different from the context that all principals face. However, in many respects, these accountability measures provide charter school principals with a clear focus and mandate for their leadership. They can align their domains of autonomy to those areas that they believe will most squarely influence student outcomes. Principal autonomy is in the service of the school's mission and, in many charter schools, this mission is aligned with accountability contexts. This is not always the case, and charter principals face tensions when balancing autonomy and accountability demands.

IMPLICATIONS FOR PRACTICE

Principals often lament that they lack the authority to focus on leadership that matters most to student achievement, yet they have all the responsibility to meet accountability goals. In charter schools, this balance between authority and responsibility may be more aligned, suggesting implications for the knowledge base and skillsets of principals. To capitalize on the autonomy afforded to them, and to meet accountability goals, charter school principals might need to develop the knowledge and skills around important domains of leadership that are not typically emphasized in traditional leadership preparation programs.

For example, principals, particularly those in independent charter schools, will need to find ways to build knowledge in areas often facilitated by district or CMO personnel, such as how to select and/or develop curricula, how to effectively screen applicants for teaching positions, and how to support and develop teachers. A few leadership preparation programs at institutions such as Loyola Marymount University and Mercer University have recognized this need, and have started to offer programs of study specifically for current or aspiring charter school leaders.

The chapter presents portraits of four charter school principals, each working to balance autonomy and accountability, all while maintaining a relentless focus on their school's mission and goals. Principals' leadership reflected varying levels of autonomy, with those in independent charter schools being afforded higher levels of autonomy than their peers in schools affiliated with a CMO, but with those in CMOs benefitting from organizational capacity and expertise. Across both types of schools, principals attempted to use the autonomy and authority of their position to adapt to change and to continue to improve.

NOTES

1. All school and personal names are pseudonyms.
2. At the time data was collected for this study, the charter schools in the state in which our study was conducted were ineligible to receive local taxes for transportation and facilities (National Alliance for Public Charter Schools, 2015).

Chapter Two

Charter School Leaders as Policy Actors

Romina Madrid Miranda and Abigail Felber-Smith

> It is 7:30 a.m. on a cool April morning, as the educators at Laker Charter School file into a classroom for a staff meeting. The school principal welcomes everyone, and invites all to recite the school mission; all begin together in unison, signaling that this is a tradition for the start of their meetings. The principal hands the meeting off to the executive director, who gives a summary of a recent school fundraiser. As she finishes, she shifts the attention back to the principal; he then invites a teacher leader (who is also a school board member) to the front. Together they facilitate a discussion about their vision for continuous improvement.

There is consensus that, while there are similarities in the overarching educational goals, leading a charter school is different from leading a traditional public school (Campbell & Gross, 2008). The opening vignette illustrates this simply in terms of the leadership structure, with teacher leaders and principals influencing policy decisions as school board members.

Running a charter school poses unique conditions for principals, which can be framed as challenges (Campbell, Gross, & Lake, 2008) and/or opportunities (Triant, 2001). In the case of stand-alone charter schools, for example, there is no central office to recruit students and teachers, secure and manage facilities, or manage school finances.

This chapter explores how two charter school principals function as policy actors. More specifically, the chapter illuminates the principals' level of influence during policy implementation—influence that is perhaps unique to stand-alone charter school principals.

Data from two schools was collected to better understand the ways in which principals and teachers made sense of the Minnesota Quality Compensation Policy (Q-Comp), and more specifically, to explore the unique role principals play in mediating teachers' sensemaking.

The Quality Compensation Policy (Q-Comp) is a statewide program that provides funding to districts and public charter schools to support alternative teacher compensation and professional development systems. In order to participate in the program, school officials submit plans regarding performance-based pay, alternative teacher salary structures, on-the-job professional development, teacher evaluations, and additional career opportunities for teachers.

Drawing on literature on the characteristics of school leadership in charter schools, sensemaking, and policy implementation, we present a qualitative case study designed to explore how principals mediate the process of teacher leadership development, a required component of Q-Comp. While there is emerging research that looks at the role of school leaders in enacting policy (Coburn, 2005; Spillane, Diamond, Burch, Hallett, Jita, & Zoltners, 2002), and the role of district leaders as policy mediators (Spillane, 1998), little is known about the role of charter school principals as policy implementers and their role as mediators of teachers' sensemaking. This chapter addresses this gap in the literature.

The following research questions guided the study:

- How do principals make sense of the Quality Compensation policy?
- How do teachers make sense of the Quality Compensation policy?
- How do principals influence teachers' sensemaking processes related to the Quality Compensation policy, in their local school context?

Findings illustrate that the charter school principals played a key role in the implementation of Q-Comp, and suggest a particular level of influence perhaps unique to stand-alone charter school principals. Principals acted as mediating agents (Louis & Robinson, 2012) in that they interpreted and influenced others' interpretation of the policy.

Principals played an active role in teachers' sensemaking via their efforts to integrate the policy into the existing school culture and, more specifically, the framework for school improvement. Principals' practices, for example, impacted not only the design and facilitation of teacher leadership development, but also the collective process of meaning making regarding the definition and value of teacher leadership in each school.

The chapter begins with a brief overview of both the literature that informed the study, and the methodology. More attention is then given to the findings and a closing discussion that includes implications for policy, practice, and research.

LITERATURE REVIEW

An underlying assumption of this study is that the unique features of a charter school likely impact the ways in which charter school principals interpret and influence policy implementation. As such, the conceptual framework that guides this chapter draws from the following bodies of literature: charter school leadership, educational policy implementation, and sensemaking. The last section on the Quality Compensation Policy (Q-comp) provides the contextual foundation for the study.

Charter School Leadership

Literature suggests that, although there are core tasks that define the principalship regardless of the organizational structure, charter school leadership has unique features. Campbell and Gross (2008) led a large-scale survey of charter school directors in seven U.S. states. They found four areas of leadership that were amplified in the charter context: creating and supporting a vision, developing and supporting human resources, sharing leadership, and using resources effectively. Little research has focused specifically on the leadership role of the charter school principal as related to policy implementation. This study attempts to, at least in part, fill that gap.

Educational Policy Implementation and Sensemaking

Educational policy implementation studies emphasize the role of *implementing agents*, exploring the process by which individuals and collectives interpret and make meaning of policies locally.

In understanding the role(s) of implementing agents, researchers have emphasized the "sensemaking process," understanding it as an active process of interpretation—not only decoding of the policy message—that draws on the individual's existing knowledge base, beliefs, and attitude (Louis & Robinson, 2012; Spillane, Reiser, and Reimer, 2002). This approach to policy research is grounded in the assumption that interpretations of the policy, and not the "objective" idea or original purpose of the policy, are implemented (Louis & Robinson, 2012). Indeed, Spillane, Reiser, and Reimer (2002) argued that in order "to explain the influences on implementation, we must explore the mechanisms by which implementing agents understand policy and attempt to connect understanding with practice" (p. 391).

Given that cognition influences behavior and practice, a central dimension of research is whether, and in what ways, implementing agents come to understand a particular policy. In addition, researchers have noted that how leaders understand a policy is partly a function of what they already value (Louis & Robinson, 2012; Spillane, 2000). In his study, Spillane (2000) investigated how district leaders understood mathematical reforms. He concluded that district leaders made sense of new policy information through their existing knowledge, and that information aligned with that knowledge had a greater weight compared to information that challenged the leaders' experiences, knowledge, and beliefs.

Louis and Robinson's (2012) study connected school leaders' sensemaking of an external accountability policy and its impact on instructional leadership. They demonstrated that the policy had a positive impact on instructional leadership—where school leaders saw the policy as aligned with their own values and preferences, and where they saw their district leaders as supportive of school-driven accountability initiatives. When one of these factors was weak or missing, leaders demonstrated more negative attitudes toward external accountability.

Coburn (2005) focused more specifically on the role of school leaders in mediating teachers' enactments of policy. She studied how principals influenced teacher learning in instructional practices regarding a particular reading policy in two elementary public schools in California. She concluded that principals influence teachers' policy enactment by shaping access to policy ideas, participating in the social process of interpretation and adaptation, and creating substantively different conditions for teacher learning in schools. These actions, in turn, are influenced by principals' understandings about reading instruction and teacher learning (Coburn, 2005).

These studies highlight the impact of principals' sensemaking in policy implementation.

The Minnesota Quality Compensation (Q-Comp) Policy

One central aim of Q-Comp is to develop teacher leadership by providing incentives to encourage teachers to improve their knowledge and instructional skills in order to improve student learning (Wahlstrom, Sheldon, & Peterson, 2006).

In 2005, the Minnesota legislature passed the Q-Comp Program based on the core principles of the Teacher Advancement Program (Center for American Progress, 2009). As a voluntary program, in 2010–2011, about 15 percent of nearly 340 school districts and 40 percent of charter schools participated in the Q-Comp program (Richert, 2011).

Districts or schools can submit a program proposal to the Minnesota Department of Education (MDE); plans must include details related to professional development opportunities, alternative teacher salary structures and performance pay, teacher evaluations, and career opportunities. If approved, schools can receive up to an additional $260 per student; this includes $169 per student in state aid and $91 per student in board-approved levy funds. As charter schools cannot levy taxes in the state of Minnesota, the state provides

$243 per student to charter schools (Minnesota Department of Education, 2016).

While the Minnesota Q-Comp policy does not prescribe how schools develop teacher leadership, it does define primary teacher leadership functions. According to the MDE's Q-Comp Application Guidelines (2015–2016), schools should develop specific teacher leadership positions that include the following responsibilities, all for the purpose of improving classroom instruction and increasing student achievement:

- Researching instructional strategies
- Conducting teacher observations and providing teacher feedback
- Coaching teachers
- Mentoring new teachers and facilitating or leading teacher teams to ensure a focus on professional development and data analysis

METHODS

The data for this qualitative case study are part of a larger five-year (2010–2015) federal grant-funded study exploring leadership development in five schools—three traditional public schools and two charter schools—located in Minnesota. A major assumption underlying the project is that a close analysis of the individual "change stories" of each school will lead to overarching themes or findings about particular practices that are associated with increased leadership capacity within schools (and ultimately, increased student learning outcomes).

Data Collection and Analysis

Here, we focused on the two charter schools—Diego Rivera Academy and Laker Charter School, because in both, the development of formal teacher leadership positions was strongly influenced by the schools' decisions to implement Q-Comp.

The primary data sources informing this chapter include interviews with administrators and teachers, and observational data collected over the course of the 2012–2013 school year. More than 30 hours were spent observing leadership team and professional learning community/peer observer meetings in each school. A total of 12 interviews, including teachers, teacher leaders, and administrators, were conducted in the spring and summer of 2013—6 in each school. All interviews were digitally recorded, transcribed, and coded.

We focused on these data points, as they are richest for exploring the stories of the localized implementation of Q-Comp and the ongoing development of formal teacher leadership. Other data, such as policy documents, a teacher survey, and interviews from previous years were used to provide context and corroborate findings.

FINDINGS

The administrators at both Laker Charter School (LCS) and Diego Rivera Academy (DRA) adhered to the requirements of Q-Comp. As mediating agents, however, the leadership practices as related to the design and implementation of the policy in their schools were unique. Administrators' practices were grounded on different interpretations of the Q-Comp, which in turn affected how teachers made sense of the teacher leadership work.

At LCS, teachers led by the principal and administrative team interpreted the Q-Comp policy as a way to augment their existing school improvement efforts. As such, the principal and administrative team designed a plan that complemented the school framework, where beliefs about collective responsibility and continuous learning were foundational. At LCS, teachers were clear about the alignment between the policy and school improvement framework. The support they required appeared more centered on the "how" of the work (mentoring, feedback, etc.) than the "what" (the teacher observation process).

At DRA, on the contrary, the principal interpreted the Q-Comp policy as "the driver of [positive] change" to the extent that peer observations were described as a specific strategy to develop teacher leadership. As such, prior to the implementation of Q-Comp, there was no visible school improvement framework but rather a variety of initiatives loosely aligned with each other. At DRA teachers were unclear about the connection between Q-Comp and the rest of improvement efforts; this lack of cohesion seemed to increase teachers' perception that assuming a leadership role was burdensome.

The story of each school (tables 2.1 and 2.2) is told in turn below; each case includes a description of how the school administrators made sense of the Q-Comp policy, implemented their Q-Comp plans, as well as a description of administrators' and teachers' perceptions of the specific teacher leadership components. The consequences of administrators' practices as policy mediators, specifically as related to teacher leadership development, are highlighted at the end of each case.

LAKER CHARTER SCHOOL

Laker Charter School (LCS) opened its doors in 1998. According to demographic and assessment data available through the Minnesota Department of Education, during the 2012–2013 school year LCS served about 300–400 students (see table 2.1).

Table 2.1. Demographics by School

School	Grades	Students	Student of Color	Free/ Red. Lunch	Prof. Reading	Prof. Math	Prof. Science
Laker Charter School	Pre-K–8	300–400	>90%	>98%	<60%	<30%	<15%
Diego Rivera Academy	Pre-K–6	300–400	>90%	>98%	<60%	<50%	<15%

In 2010, the LCS leaders decided to implement a turnaround model with the assumption that such change would support their chances of receiving a School Improvement Grant (SIG). As such, they replaced approximately 50 percent of their staff, including the principal.[1]

The new principal developed a framework (with support from the administrative team) to guide school improvement efforts, referred to as the "Three Pillars." The pillars referred to the following:

- Focused professional learning communities (PLCs)
- Common school-wide and classroom practices
- Ongoing feedback and support

The principal was purposefully transparent about his vision for school improvement—he wanted all staff members to understand why they were doing what they were doing.

Q-Comp Policy at LCS

The design and implementation of the Q-Comp plan were intentionally integrated into the school improvement philosophy. At the time of the study, LCS was in the first year of Q-Comp policy implementation. The proposal planning process took about two months and, according to an administrator, did not require much extra work mainly because it reflected activities for the development of teacher leadership positions already planned as part of ongoing school improvement efforts.

In this way, goals, procedures, members, measures, deadlines, and expected outcomes were already defined, at least by administrators, via existing school improvement plans and documents.

Since school administrators viewed Q-Comp as supporting existing plans, they framed it as such to the broader staff. In other words, they mediated a

Table 2.2. Demographics by School

School	Asian	Hispanic	Black	White	Amer. Indian	English Learners	Spec. Educ.
Laker Charter School	35%	33%	24%	7%	2%	62%	11%
Diego Rivera Academy	3%	89%	4%	1%	3%	80%	11%

message of the Q-Comp program as a support mechanism, not "another new thing."

Regarding teacher leadership, the Q-Comp program at LCS defined five formal teacher leadership positions. The primary role of the teacher leaders (in addition to their classroom responsibilities) was to conduct two or three peer observations over the course of the school year. The observations included a pre-conference, an observation, and a post-conference.

Additional responsibilities included serving as leaders of their professional learning communities (PLCs) and attending sessions designed to develop their leadership skills, particularly as related to peer coaching. Those were scheduled as needed (e.g., debrief after a round of peer observations). In order to fulfill these responsibilities, teacher leaders needed to work extra hours, although in some cases they were pulled out of their classes.

At LCS, neither teachers nor administrators considered the Q-Comp policy a driver of change. Instead, they saw themselves as leading the change at the school; the policy was described as supporting, formalizing, or complementing existing improvement initiatives. Administrators and teachers, for example, seemed to find value in the Q-Comp policy in that it provided resources such as funding to implement their improvement plans.

The principal described this by saying, "I think for us Q-Comp was kind of a formality but we were doing all, we would have been doing all these pieces regardless if we had it or not. So, for us . . . it's an opportunity to get some additional funds but, . . . I wouldn't say that was our driving force."

Further, the quote above reflects the intentional ways in which the principal integrated the policy into the guiding improvement framework.

Implementation of Q-Comp

As required by the Q-Comp policy, the teacher leader positions had to be formally posted; any teacher could apply and be interviewed for the position. Administrators explained the ease in choosing the teacher leaders; those that applied were the most experienced teachers within each PLC team.

The details of implementation were negotiated with teacher leaders; they worked closely with the curriculum and assessment coordinator to design the best strategy to implement peer observations. Together they decided that the teacher leaders would observe teachers outside of their respective PLCs team. They wanted both to avoid placing unnecessary strain on existing relationships, and promote greater vertical alignment of teaching practices.

Initially, the peer observers did not use a formal observation rubric; instead, pre-observation conferences were used to identify an area in which a particular teacher wanted feedback. Later, under guidance from administrators, it was decided that teacher leaders would use the same observation tool that administrators used for the remaining rounds of observations during the school year to support common practices throughout the school.

Along with intentionally creating the "sense of transparency" among teachers, the principal saw the observation process as a tool for establishing common expectations of effective teacher practices. Again, the principal offered a clear sense of direction, and established core values that characterized the work that teacher leaders were doing.

In addition to peer observations, the administrators at LCS developed a strategy for supporting the peer observers in their learning as peer coaches. That is, another observer was invited to attend the post-observation conferences; this person's role was to scribe the conversation and then meet with the peer observer to reflect on their facilitation and coaching skills. This strategy underscores the culture of professional learning throughout the school. Moreover, it supported an equal distribution of power between the observers and those being observed, positioning everyone as a learner.

LCS was focused on developing a culture oriented to continuous improvement, and the principal was purposeful in developing systems to collectively build the capacity of all staff members. Therefore, the Q-Comp policy was viewed as a vehicle for developing teacher leadership throughout the school.

Not Individual but School-wide Goals

Consistent with the school framework of collective responsibility, the criteria for distributing the policy's monetary bonuses emphasized school-wide goals. The largest percentage of the money was allocated according to school-wide reading and math assessment scores on state assessments, and on professional learning community team goals. The lowest percentage was allocated based on the individual teacher evaluation conducted by a school administrator. Lastly, the principal valued transparency and, as such, pointed out the importance of all people knowing who is involved in Q-Comp and, therefore, who was eligible for the monetary bonuses.

Teachers' Sensemaking

In general, teachers at LCS perceived the school initiatives as positive and as facilitating changes in their practices. They did, however, voice mixed feelings, particularly associated with perceived pressures for change.

First, teachers saw the inclusion of the Q-Comp policy as a tool to enhance teacher leadership. In addition, teacher leadership development was viewed as a way to build a bridge between teachers and administrators, which fostered the creation of coherence within the school as a whole. One teacher expressed, "I feel like the decision was made to have these teacher leaderships to kind of, build in, like, that standing area in the middle. . . . Before it was just such disconnect, and I think it was also affecting teachers . . . I know one goal is like, make teachers feel more comfortable with both the process and understanding that we are one as a whole."

Second, teachers believed that formalizing the teacher leadership work, specifically in terms of peer observation processes, was important for improving teachers' instructional practices across the school. Specifically, they referred to the possibility of incorporating clear criteria and guidelines about their teaching practices. A teacher leader said, "I think the biggest success is that teachers are able to reflect back on their teaching. And we used the guidelines. We looked at the classroom management. We looked at their instruction delivery. We looked at students' participation and we use those guidelines to not evaluate, but to reflect."

While the data suggests that teachers were clear on the "what" and "why" of the work, some teachers experienced a level of uncertainty regarding the "how." Such concerns were framed in terms of the overall school improvement efforts, and not necessarily perceived as caused by the Q-Comp policy.

One of the most important concerns was the sense of being "overwhelmed," caused by the tension between urgency and support. This also relates to the idea that making changes is a process, organized in different levels or stages; change is not immediate. A teacher captured this sentiment: "I feel like some of us are kind of, then, secretly almost feeling like we need to make magic."

Teacher leaders affirmed that time out of their own classroom was one of the most difficult aspects of the leadership work. One shared, "So, that [leaving the classroom] was a really big challenge for me because I love to be in the classroom and anytime I have to be taken out, I get very anxious. I like to know what's going on; [know if] my plans are getting done the way that I wanted them to get done." The teacher's words suggest that the feeling of uncertainty that goes with leaving the classroom was another source of stress for teacher leaders.

The School Leader as a Sensemaker

Teachers and formal teacher leaders agreed that school administrators played a key role in integrating the Q-Comp components into their existing work, as outlined by the Three Pillars framework (i.e., focused PLCs, common practices, and feedback and support). At the foundation of the framework was a belief in continuous learning for all, including those in formal leadership positions.

The role of principal was critical in developing and strengthening this culture of learning. For example, the principal emphasized the importance of observation and reflective dialogues about one's practice as critical for improving instruction. Therefore, peer-observer activities of Q-Comp were embedded in a cyclical process of teacher observation, modeling, and coaching that was already in place.

School administrators, with input from teacher leaders, were intentional about introducing the peer observation process as a peer-to-peer learning process rather than an expert-novice relationship. In this way, the process of evaluation was framed as a learning opportunity—the goal being teacher reflection and learning, rather than teacher evaluation. One administrator shared, "Before our first peer coaching conversation, as I was talking to staff and informing them about the process, the piece the [teacher] leads really wanted me to reinforce was that they're not there to evaluate or to judge what you're doing, they're there just as a person to guide you through that reflection... I think that was really helpful for teachers."

Teachers' sensemaking of the peer observation as a process of learning was also fostered by the fact that there was no direct link between the observation and the distribution of Q-Comp monies.

The idea of incorporating a second observer (scribe) in the post-conference as a means of providing feedback to the peer observer is another example of how administrators made sense of the observation process. Their belief that all could and should learn from the observation work was clear. One teacher leader shared, "I noticed how much the effect of scribing had on us, on things that we weren't necessarily conscious of ourselves." This teacher leader went on to say that it was very helpful to have "another set of eyes," and to have time to reflect with someone else about the feedback she was giving to her peers.

The case of LCS exemplifies the value of deliberately implementing the policy so that the work coheres with existing school goals. The principal took the lead; both administrators and teacher leaders, however, were influential in defining specific aspects of the implementation, which contributed to the sensemaking process for all staff. They guided others in connecting the peer observations to the Three Pillars framework, and helped to interpret Q-Comp activities as a learning process for all.

As a result, LCS teachers seemed to describe their work in terms of the overall school improvement efforts, rarely discussing the Q-Comp plan in isolation (unless prompted by the interviewers). Similarly, their concerns were based on feeling pressured to perform at a certain level as a consequence of the overall school improvement efforts, and not necessarily rooted in the Q-Comp plan itself.

DIEGO RIVERA ACADEMY

Diego Rivera Academy (DRA) opened in 2001 and served about 300–400 students in 2013 (see table 2.1). The school was deliberate about understanding the needs and assets of the community it serves. DRA founders, for example, created a formal administrative team that, at the time of this study, included the executive director and principal, and a director of family and community engagement.

Q-Comp Policy at DRA

At the time of the study, DRA was in the third year of implementation of the Q-Comp policy. At the beginning, the principal and instructional specialist wrote the Q-Comp plan. In their third year, however, the task of creating the Q-Comp proposal was assumed by the instructional specialist and the peer observers. Minimal, if any, changes were made to the formal Q-Comp plan over the course of the three years.

Implementation of Q-Comp

The Q-Comp plan centered on the development of a team of peer observers (i.e., teacher leaders). School administrators facilitated a peer observer selection process annually, and any teacher interested in the position could apply. As in the case of LCS, the roles and responsibilities for the peer observer lead positions were in addition to full-time classroom teaching responsibilities.

The peer observers conducted two observations annually. Each observation cycle included a pre- and post-conference, a 40- to 50-minute classroom observation, and the completion of a feedback report based on the observation rubric. The peer observers met weekly before school.

The peer observers also served as leaders of their professional learning communities (PLCs). With the development of a school-wide leadership team (LT) in 2012–2013, the peer observers' responsibilities extended to the LT. In addition to the six peer observers (five of whom were classroom teachers, and one the full-time instructional specialist), additional staff members and the principal served on the LT. The overlap in roles and responsibilities for peer observers was deliberate—the underlying assumption was that leading PLCs, conducting peer observations, and serving on the LT would create greater alignment within and across the continuous improvement efforts.

Another part of the Q-Comp plan was the development of a small mentorship program. While this took different forms over the years, during the third year there was one half-time mentor teacher. Her primary responsibilities were to support new teachers in acclimating to DRA's culture, and improve instructional practices. The mentor position was partially funded through Q-Comp.

Individual and School-wide Goals

The performance pay component of DRA's Q-Comp plan was based on three goals: one school-wide goal (based on the state standardized assessments), one grade-level goal (based on grade-level assessments), and the third was based on the results of an individual's peer observation. Teachers had to earn an average of 3 on a 4-point rubric (across 16 components) over the 2 peer observation cycles in order to receive the bonus pay.

The Value of Q-Comp

The principal and several formal leaders described the Q-Comp policy as a "driver of change" in the school. In the quote below, the principal underscores the critical role of Q-Comp to the development of common expectations regarding teaching practices.

> *Interviewer:* How do you see it fitting into the larger change efforts of this school?
>
> *Principal:* Huge. It's probably been the biggest thing that's ever happened here. Just to have peer observations.
>
> *Interviewer:* What do you think is the greatest consequence of that?
>
> *Principal:* I think you see improved instruction, more consistent instruction, people are getting into their brains as to what the rubric looks like, what a good lesson looks like.

Teacher leaders valued the fact that Q-Comp elevated the teacher leadership and legitimized the position within the school. The instructional specialist, who was in charge of overseeing the Q-Comp plan, explained the policy's role in the creation of teacher leader positions at DRA: "Prior to Q-Comp, there weren't really formal teacher leaders. There were no peer observers or peer observation. . . . The money helped to legitimize a full-time instructional specialist and also to augment the salaries of five peer observers."

In addition to valuing the teacher leadership components, the principal also spoke about Q-Comp in terms of the economic component. That is, she named teacher retention as a priority, and referenced Q-Comp as a tool for boosting her efforts: "The initiation of Q-Comp at DRA was purely to get more money for the teachers. The pay discrepancy between large districts and charters is incredible, so I thought this might be a way to help with some sort of equity."

Teachers and principal valued the Q-Comp policy for the possibility of incrementing teachers' pay. One teacher explained, "and of course the money with Q-Comp, I mean . . . I'm not going to lie, this is the best thing ever because we're not going to get any more money."

Teachers' Sensemaking

Teachers and teacher leaders agreed that changes derived from Q-Comp plan were positive overall. They talked about the role of the observations as important in creating consistency in teacher practices and in providing opportunities to learn about best practices that did not exist before.

However, several teachers and teacher leaders acknowledged increased workloads for teacher leaders, stressors on teacher-teacher relationships, and tensions around the allocation of monies. One teacher commented, "I really think the balance of being a teacher and a teacher leader is a little bit harder. That's where it gets a little much. Like, when I was a mentor I finally just said, 'I am not going to do this next year. I need time to be in my classroom.'"

This sentiment could, at least in part, be attributed to the peer observation process, which was perceived as cumbersome, overly formal, and rigid. The observation cycle was described by some as being overly prescriptive. One teacher leader shared, "It's hard because I feel like, what they ask you to do in that lesson is not humanly possible for every lesson you teach; you know? . . . It's so much paperwork . . . they [teachers] feel like they have to do more work." The work with the observation rubric was perceived as exhausting and not well suited to capturing the dynamism of the teaching process. Thus, at least for some, the whole process was discouraging.

Another source of conflict for teachers was the criteria for allocating the Q-Comp money. Some teachers perceived that the relation between the amount of work and the payment was inadequate. One teacher leader explained, "I think the observations are worth it, but when you look at it from the money perspective, I mean after taxes it's nothing [laughter]. . . . When you get observed, you probably have five to six hours of paperwork just for the observation . . . the paperwork is intense."

Others viewed the allocation of money based on individual scores (on the peer observation rubric) as a threat to continuous improvement. Thus, rather than using the observation as a tool for professional learning, some teachers seemed to acutely focus on the scores and whether these would translate into money.

In sum, teachers acknowledged that the creation of formal teacher leadership roles through Q-Comp had both positive and negative consequences. They valued the teacher leadership opportunities, and the establishment of school-wide instructional expectations. They also perceived negative consequences in terms of an increased workload and the confusion surrounding what they depicted as several stand-alone improvement initiatives. In addition, the allocation of the "bonus" money based on individual scores on the peer observation rubric created additional stress for some teachers.

Making Sense of the Q-Comp Policy

Data suggested a disagreement between how the principal and the teachers made sense of the Q-Comp policy at DRA. The principal, for example, expressed having a strong sense of clarity and connection regarding the school's various improvement efforts. She noted, "All of the different grants that we have, I don't see them bumping heads with each other; I see them as a nice fit. This is clearly curricular. [Another grant] is clearly about building teacher leadership."

Teachers, however, expressed confusion about all the initiatives at DRA. They noted the need for more clarification about how the various initiatives connected with a singular school improvement vision. In tune with teachers' perceptions, the instructional specialist argued that the diversity of initiatives in place made it difficult to see the big picture.

The principal, aware of this situation, shared a visual map that the LT created to support greater coherence around school improvement initiatives. In describing it, she said, "We created it [a visual map of the various school initiatives and supports] and the LT brought it to the whole staff for revision, brought it back to the LT for more discussion, brought it back to the staff for more revision until it was finalized. . . . But people still don't get it." One interpretation of the confusion is that the administrator(s) failed to create a clear picture and a collective "sense" about school improvement efforts.

DRA's story illustrates the efforts and challenges in developing and sustaining teacher leadership as part of the Q-Comp policy. The principal saw the Q-Comp policy as a driving force in the school's improvement efforts for various reasons—the impact on teacher leadership development, the creation of greater coherence across teaching practices, and the potential for additional pay. However, to varying degrees, teachers' sensemaking confirms the lack of articulation and clarity around multiple initiatives for improvement.

Teachers felt overwhelmed by the amount of work, and frustrated with the criteria for allocating Q-Comp money.

DISCUSSION

This chapter explores the roles of two charter school principals as policy actors. Evidence suggests that both principals acted as mediating agents (Louis & Robinson, 2012)—they played an active role in integrating Q-Comp into existing school improvement narratives, shaping the way in which Q-Comp was implemented, and influencing how teachers made sense of the teacher leadership work.

Sensemaking is important in that how one interprets new information directly influences actions (Spillane, Reiser, & Reimer, 2002). The two principals differed in how they made sense of the policy. At LCS, the principal, and the administrative team interpreted the policy via the existing culture of continuous improvement and collective responsibility put forth by the Three Pillars framework. The allocation of Q-Comp money based on team and school-wide goals was coherent with this framework. Similarly, administrators purposefully designed and implemented their peer observation system as a tool to support continuous learning for all.

At DRA, the Q-Comp policy was discussed more in isolation, as a set of independent initiatives. One explanation for this is that, at the time Q-Comp was implemented, there was no dominant vision of school improvement. This matches the principal's description of the Q-Comp plan as a driver of change. Indeed, the need to enhance clarity among staff about the various initiatives was a permanent concern for the Leadership Team. Furthermore, the attention to the rubric and the comprehensive observation cycle, in conjunction with the strategy for allocating Q-Comp monies seemed to focus the work on the individual.

In this study, the principals functioned as policy actors as they mediated teachers' sensemaking about the policy in relation to broader school-wide improvement efforts. Similar to previous findings (Coburn 2005; Louis & Robinson, 2012), the authors found that principals' understanding of the policy along with subsequent action shaped others' sensemaking, particularly regarding teacher leadership development (as part of the Q-Comp policy).

Teachers at LCS rarely referred to the Q-Comp policy itself, but rather described practices in the context of the overall cycle of improvement, which included classroom observations, modeling, and coaching. Likewise, teachers' concerns were articulated around the pressure imposed by the overall improvement effort, and not necessarily by the Q-Comp policy. The administrative team seemed to achieve a cohesive vision of school improvement.

Although DRA was in the third year of implementation, teachers' voices conveyed less clarity about the overall school improvement vision. As a result, more effort from administrators was allocated to support others' sensemaking (compared to LCS). In addition, at DRA teachers and teacher leaders disagreed with the principal's idea of linking the individual results of the peer evaluation to an economic reward; this decision seemed to contribute to teachers interpreting the Q-Comp policy as a source of stress and pressure.

In other words, to the extent DRA teachers interpreted the Q-Comp policy as an independent initiative, the goals of developing teacher leadership for bolstering a culture of continuous improvement and creating coherence of diverse improvement initiatives seemed to be in process—not yet achieved.

Evidence suggests that an intentionally designed and clearly articulated school improvement framework facilitated teachers' sensemaking and, thus, the implementation of the teacher leadership components of the Q-Comp policy.

One limitation of this study is that it was not designed as a comparison between traditional public school principals and charter school principals. One might assume, however, that the structure of these stand-alone charter schools as compared to traditional public schools allowed that the charter school principals played a more direct role in teachers' sensemaking, in that they did not have an intermediate actor(s) such as management organizations (MOs) and/or district leaders.

Implications for Practice and Research

There are several implications related to the role that charter school principals play as policy actors. First, principals play a critical role in preparing the setting for the inclusion of policies, by intentionally crafting coherence among multiple initiatives. More research is needed to better understand how the role of school leaders as policy actors might vary depending on the organizational structure (e.g., charter management organizations, traditional public schools).

As key policy actors, principals need to filter through and prioritize which policies fit best with the school culture and existing school improvement efforts. In this study, administrators acquired information about Q-Comp, and were aware of the potential benefits prior to submitting a proposal.

This study reinforces previous studies (Campbell & Gross, 2008) about the important role of charter school principals in creating and supporting a vision about school purposes and pathways to growth. It emphasizes the role of the principal in facilitating a coherent vision of school improvement. Evidence shows that the principal's role is not only helping teachers make sense of the policy itself, but also supporting them in navigating the implementation stage. Principals must develop a realistic plan for implementing the policy—one that considers the range of initiatives in the school.

Regarding the development of teacher leadership, this study highlights the need for continuous support for teachers taking on leadership roles. In both cases, principals provided ongoing opportunities for building the leadership capacity of the teachers. For example, at LCS, the principal brought in a consultant to coach teacher leaders, and they continuously refined their skills for guiding learning conversations with their peers.

Despite principals purposely providing ongoing learning opportunities for teacher leaders, teachers voiced feeling overwhelmed by the demands of being a classroom teacher and a formal teacher leader. At DRA, where the teachers assumed the details for organizing the work, there seemed to be more concerns or pushback than at LCS, where the administrative team seemed to share more of the work.

While some might argue that increasing teacher voice and input would lead to greater overall satisfaction and outcomes, the data here seems to suggest the importance of finding a balance, particularly when teacher leaders are also full-time classroom teachers.

In sum, in an effort to develop teacher leadership, principals must delineate opportunities to build the particular leadership skills required for these positions. Moreover, data suggests that there is a permanent need for supporting teachers in the challenges they face when accepting leadership roles in addition to their classroom responsibilities. Charter school principals play a key role in this work.

Moreover, in exploring the role of charter school principals as policy actors, this analysis focuses on administrators' and teachers' processes of sensemaking. Future research is needed to better understand how sensemaking processes influence teachers' instructional practices and, thus, impact student learning outcomes.

Although the importance of permanent support for teachers in leadership roles was highlighted, we did not explore in detail the principals' strategies to support teachers. Therefore, further studies are needed to illuminate the most effective strategies for addressing these issues with teachers.

Regarding the different philosophical underpinnings of teacher leadership development found in each school (one that emphasized teachers taking greater responsibility versus one in which the principal and the core team led the change), future research might look at the longer-term implications of these different approaches on teacher leadership development.

NOTE

1. In the end, they were not awarded a SIG.

Chapter Three

How Charter School Principals Use Teacher Evaluation Systems

David B. Reid

Within the field of education, there is perhaps no more polarizing current issue than teacher evaluation policies. The polarizing nature of these policies is due in part to the increasing acknowledgement that teacher quality can positively impact student outcomes, such as achievement and attendance (Chetty, Friedman, & Rockoff, 2014; Rockoff, 2004) and in part to research suggesting teacher evaluation systems have historically done a poor job distinguishing teacher performance (U.S. Department of Education, 2009; Weisberg, Sexton, Mulhern, & Keeling, 2009).

In 2009, the Race to the Top initiative incentivized states to create more rigorous teacher evaluation systems that provided better information on what makes a high-quality teacher. As a result, since 2009 more than two-thirds of states have made significant changes to how teachers are evaluated (Center for Public Education, 2013). This nationwide reform effort has resulted in schools, principals, and teachers having to learn, interpret, and make sense of new teacher evaluation systems at a rapid pace.

School principals play a crucial role in how policies and systems, including teacher evaluation systems, play out in practice (Halverson, Kelley, & Kimball, 2004; Rigby, 2015). How principals interpret, communicate, and ultimately carry out new teacher evaluation systems has great implications for how these systems are used. While principals have always assumed the responsibility of evaluating their staff, the stakes are now higher for this process because in many cases, new teacher evaluation systems have tied a teacher's evaluation score to career-defining decisions, such as hiring, firing, and tenure.

To date, much of the research on how principals make sense of evaluating their teaching staff has focused on principals in traditional public school settings (Grissom & Loeb, forthcoming; Halverson et al., 2004; Kraft & Gilmour, 2015; Rigby, 2015). Less is known about how charter school principals navigate this important process. This distinction is important because in many cases, the challenges charter school principals face when evaluating their staff differ from the challenges experienced by principals in traditional settings.

For example, because charter school principals lack the support of a district or central office, they are often tasked with adopting or creating their own teacher evaluation system. Additionally, while traditional public school principals can rely on district or central offices for support and clarification regarding how to best use teacher evaluation systems, charter school principals do not have this same support and are often left to implement these complex systems on their own.

Another challenge that charter school principals typically face is a tendency toward higher teacher turnover and less experienced teachers than their traditional public school principal peers (Miron & Applegate, 2007; Stuit & Smith, 2012) and, as a result, they must evaluate new and less experienced teachers more often. When using teacher evaluations as a means of accountability and potential dismissal of ineffective teachers, charter principals must consider such things as teacher recruitment and hiring, or even whether they will have enough qualified applicants to fill vacated positions.

Traditional public school principals generally have the support of district or central offices to manage these responsibilities. One final important difference between teacher evaluations in traditional public schools and charter schools is the fact that many traditional public school districts, particularly larger school districts, have taken steps to better standardize the evaluation process in an effort to ensure fairness, as evaluations are often compared across entire districts and used for human capital decisions. Evaluations in charter schools are not used for comparing teachers at different schools (in most circumstances).

Charter school principal cognition and sensemaking of teacher evaluation systems may also differ from that of principals in traditional public schools. For example, traditional public school principals may draw on their informal networks, such as other principals within the district or other district personnel, to make sense of how to use their district's teacher evaluation system. Charter school principals are generally more isolated, relying on their own experiences, knowledge, and beliefs when making sense of how to best use these systems.

Additionally, traditional public school principals may receive directives from a district or central office, including precise instructions for implementing teacher evaluations, communicating these systems to their teachers, and documenting all aspects of the evaluation process. Charter school principals are left to make sense of these things on their own. In short, traditional public school principals' cognition is, at least in part, influenced by district-wide thinking and district initiatives, whereas charter school principals' cognition is more likely influenced by their individual experiences and beliefs and/or the mission of their individual schools (Gawlik, 2015).

This comparative case study followed two charter school principals in Michigan as they navigated the process of evaluating their teaching staffs. The research questions that guided this work were: (1) How do charter school principals use teacher evaluation systems? And (2) What factor(s) impact how charter school principals evaluate the teachers in their building? The data collected include:

- Interviews with principals
- Observations of daily principal practices (including formal observations of teachers and pre- and post-observation conferences between principals and teachers)
- Principal observation notes and final teacher evaluation scores/summaries
- A questionnaire completed by the principals

The purpose of this study was to collect and describe responses and actions of charter school principals by documenting their perceptions, beliefs, attitudes, roles, and procedures regarding how they think about and evaluate the teachers in their respective buildings.

REVIEW OF RELATED LITERATURE

The Role of Principals as Leaders of Teacher Evaluation

While early research suggested that principals lacked the power and influence to change school and teacher practices (Bidwell, 2001), more recent research suggests principals play a key role in how initiatives and reforms play out in practice (Coburn, 2005; Gawlik, 2012). How principals think about and implement education reforms is of particular importance, as research indicates that principals are second only to teachers as the educational resource that can most positively impact student outcomes, such as learning, increased attendance, and increased graduation rates (Leithwood, Seashore-Louis, Anderson, & Wahlstrom, 2004; Louis, Leithwood, Wahlstrom, & Anderson, 2010).

One specific way all school principals can positively impact student outcomes is by hiring, developing, and retaining high-quality teachers (Davis, Darling-Hammond, LaPointe, & Meyerson, 2005; Ladd, 2011; Leithwood, Harris, & Hopkins, 2008). Research is growing on the role principals play in cultivating their teaching staff, but there is a lack of attention given to charter school principals.

While their traditional public school peers have the support of central offices for things such as managing buildings, managing personnel, and student recruiting, charter school principals must balance normal job responsibilities, such as managing a school and serving as the instructional leader, while also taking on these additional responsibilities (Bickmore & Dowell, 2011; Campbell & Gross, 2008).

Charter school principals are typically granted greater latitude in the operation of their school than principals in traditional settings (Bickmore & Dowell, 2011; Dressler, 2001), including greater autonomy in creating and spending the school budget, setting standards and curriculum for instruction, and the overall structure and emphasis of the school day (Gawlik, 2008). Finally, and of particular importance to this study, charter school principals typically experience greater freedom in hiring, evaluating, and retaining teachers than principals in traditional public school settings (Allen & Consoletti, 2010).

The Co-Evolution of Teacher Evaluation Policies and the Role of Principals

One specific responsibility of the school leader is to evaluate teaching staff, which principals have done in some form for the past century. Early research showed principals played a more hands-off role during evaluations, as principals rarely evaluated classroom instruction and instead completed a checklist of teacher responsibilities, including items such as whether a teacher showed up to work on time (Wise, Darling-Hammond, McLaughlin, & Bernstein, 1985). However, as teacher evaluation systems transitioned into more high-stakes policies, principals began to take a more active role in the evaluation process.

Over the past several decades, principals have been asked to become competent evaluators of classroom instruction and provide meaningful and critical feedback to teachers, taking on the dual role of coach and evaluator (Duke & Stiggins, 1986, 1990). More recently, principals have been tasked with taking on the role of an instructional leader, where the principal is charged with supporting teacher instruction and is held accountable, along with teachers, for student learning (Blasé, Blasé, & Phillips, 2010; Smylie, 2010).

As most schools currently use rigorous teacher evaluation systems, which typically include a student achievement–based component as well as an observational component with a detailed and structured observation rubric, the role of the principal in the evaluation process is much more defined than in previous years (Goldring et al., 2015). For example, in most situations principals are given specific directions for how and when to observe teachers, how to score teachers, and how to provide feedback to teachers (Goldring et al., 2015).

In sum, the role of the principal in teacher evaluations has changed significantly as the landscape for teacher evaluation policy has evolved. Now, in most cases, part of a principals' own evaluation includes student performance data and information on how they evaluate their staff. As a result, principals are incentivized to take a more active role in the evaluation and development of the teachers in their building.

Given the research suggesting that principals make many school-based decisions, including human capital decisions, based on teacher evaluation scores (Goldring et al., 2015; Hanushek & Rivkin, 2010; Jacob, 2011), additional research is needed to see what factors impact how principals think about their current role in the teacher evaluation process. This research is particularly needed in the understudied subgroup of charter school principals.

The Role of Principal Cognition During Teacher Evaluations

Weatherley and Lipsky (1977) stressed the importance of "street-level bureaucrats"—the individuals who impact how policies are ultimately implemented. These individuals and their cognition, including their beliefs, skills, will, resources, time, context, and capacity, impact how policies look in practice. While principals are experiencing more clarity and structure with regard to how they are to evaluate their teaching staff, principal cognition still greatly impacts how these policies play out in practice (Coburn, 2005; Halverson et al., 2004; Spillane, Reiser, & Reimer, 2002).

Several studies have looked at how cognition impacts teacher evaluation policy implementation, concluding that principals navigate trade-offs and adjust and negotiate the demands of evaluating teachers in their buildings based on their prior knowledge and personal context (Halverson & Clifford, 2006; Halverson et al., 2004; Rigby, 2015). However, this research comes primarily from the traditional public school context.

Including the perspective of charter school principals has the potential to further our understanding of how principal cognition impacts teacher evaluation policy implementation. By looking at the case of charter school principals, we can test the applicability of some of these previous traditional public school principal findings and see how, if at all, the charter school principal perspective compares to that of traditional pubic school principals.

METHODOLOGY

Research Design

This case study of two charter school principals in Michigan is part of a larger study, which includes nine traditional public school principals. Case studies have proven to be a good design to see how multiple variables interact in an environment (Miles & Huberman, 1994; Yin, 2009). Specifically, this research took on the design of a comparative case study. A comparative case study approach is particularly useful when trying to understand how context influences the way a policy or system plays out in practice (Berg, 2007). Charter school principals' thinking and enactment of teacher evaluation systems is the primary unit of analysis in this work.

The goal of this study was to better understand how charter school principals make sense of teacher evaluations and, ultimately, what factors influence how they evaluate their teachers. In an effort to best address these research questions, this study purposefully selected two charter school principals who met four criteria.

First, the principals were required to be located in the same state, as charter laws greatly impact how charter schools may operate from state to state (Bickmore & Dowell, 2011). Second, the principals solicited for this study had to have either none to four years of experience or eight or more years of experience, in an effort to compare principals with low and high experience levels. Research shows that, much like teachers, as principals gain experience they are better able to secure relationships with staff, improve staff effectiveness, fully implement policies and practices, and make significant education improvements (Louis et al., 2010).

Third, as it is well established that outside accountability pressures influence how principals make sense of and implement policies (Coburn, 2005; Gawlik, 2012; Halverson & Clifford, 2006; Rigby, 2015), participants were selected from two different accountability ratings based on the 2014 Michigan Schools Accountability Scorecard. Briefly, the Michigan Schools Accountability Scorecard combines student assessment data with graduation and attendance rates, and compliance with federal and state laws. The purpose of the scorecard is to give the state, districts, schools, parents, and the public a way to see how schools are performing in each of the areas previously mentioned.

These scorecards replaced No Child Left Behind's (NCLB) annual yearly progress (AYP) reports, and the scorecard system is currently a good gauge to see which schools in Michigan are facing the most accountability pressures. In 2014, schools in Michigan received either green (highest), lime, yellow, orange, or red (lowest) ratings. The principals in this study represent schools at two different rating levels (lime and red).

Finally, principals were solicited in an effort to get a variety of charter school types (independent charter schools, which are governed by their board and authorizer, and Charter/Education Management Organizations, which are governed by their board, authorizer, and the company that typically operates multiple schools). Complete information on this study's participants can be found in table 3.1.

Data Collection

Case studies typically draw information from sources such as interviews, direct observations, participant observations, documentation, archival records, and artifacts (Yin, 2009). The collection of multiple sources of data is done in an effort to triangulate and corroborate findings (Yin, 2009). This study relied on four sources of information: a questionnaire, interviews, observations, and artifacts.

Questionnaire

The questionnaire used for this study was administered at the beginning of data collection in the spring of 2016. The purpose of the questionnaire was twofold: First, the questionnaire was used as a screening process to get background data to ensure that the principals met the aforementioned criteria. Additionally, the questionnaire was used to generate some of the interview questions used in this study.

Principal Interviews

Each participant in this study was interviewed three times. The interviews occurred in a one-on-one setting, and focused on each principal's' experiences and perceptions of using teacher evaluation systems. Interviews were conducted in the spring of 2016, when the principals were in the middle of evaluating their teaching staff.

The purpose of the interviews was to better understand how principals were making sense of their school's teacher evaluation system, and what

Table 3.1. School Type, School Rating, Principal Experience

Principal	Charter Type	School Rating	Years as Principal	Years at Current School	Years as Teacher	Level of Education
Ms. Cohen	Independ.	Red	>10	3	6	MA
Mr. Sherman	CMO	Lime	4	4	1	MA

factors influenced principal thinking and enactment of these systems. The interviews, each lasting between 30 and 60 minutes, were conducted over a period of two months and were recorded and transcribed.

Observations

Each principal was observed while conducting an official teacher observation used for a teacher's final evaluation score. Additionally, one principal, Ms. Cohen (all names are pseudonyms) was observed at the subsequent teacher evaluation post-conference. The second principal, Mr. Sherman, only required a post-conference if requested by either the principal or the teacher. In this case, neither the principal nor the teacher requested a post-conference after the official observation. Instead, the third interview conducted with Mr. Sherman asked additional questions about what typically takes place during these post-conferences when they do occur.

During the observations, field notes were taken, focusing specifically on the behaviors, conversations, questions, and dialogue of principals with teachers. After completing these field notes, conversations were conducted with both the principal and the teacher to ensure an accurate representation of their interaction was captured by the researcher.

The purpose of the observations was to better understand how principals observe teachers in practice, and how principals and teachers communicate about the evaluation process. Additionally, in qualitative research it is important to observe people in their natural environments in order to gain a deeper and different perspective on how these individuals act while performing a task (Yin, 2009).

Specific Teacher Evaluation Documents

School-specific teacher evaluation documents were gathered from the principals. Specifically, each school's observation protocol, based in part on the Danielson Framework, were collected. While these observation protocols had components similar to the traditional Danielson Framework observation protocol, each school and principal adapted the actual protocol.

The feedback each principal provided their teachers after the observed lesson was also collected. In each case, this feedback was delivered in a school-created document and sent to the teachers via email. The purpose of collecting these documents was to better understand what these principals would be looking for during teacher observations, and to better understand the type of feedback principals were giving teachers.

Additionally, this information was collected in an effort to see what these principals noticed during teacher observations, and if and when this information was addressed during teacher evaluation post-conferences and in principal feedback to teachers. Finally, teacher evaluation scores and summaries were collected from each principal. The purpose of collecting these documents was to see additional feedback principals provided to their teachers, and to see the final teacher evaluation rating these teachers received.

Participants and School Context

Ms. Cohen worked in traditional public schools for almost 20 years as a teacher and administrator. During these two decades, she worked in a large urban area and in high-performing schools. Near the end of her tenure in traditional public schools, Ms. Cohen decided she wanted to open a high-quality charter school for students in the same large urban area. After several years of planning, Ms. Cohen's vision became a reality, and her new charter school opened. She has served as the school's principal for its three years of existence.

Along with her authorizer and two other members of her leadership team, Ms. Cohen had a great amount of influence in the design and adoption of her school's current teacher evaluation system. Ms. Cohen described her school's evaluation system as a variation of Charlotte Danielson's Framework for Teaching, including using a similar observation rubric and having similar evaluation events, such as a pre-conference, official observation, and post-conference. Per state requirements, 25 percent of a teacher's evaluation score was based on student achievement data. This 25 percent came from school-created assessments and was based on students' growth during the school year.

When asked how she was trained on the Danielson Framework, Ms. Cohen said, "A trainer for the Danielson model [came to our school]. He was the one that said that you should leave it the way it is. It's pure. Don't take from it. I didn't listen." Ms. Cohen also noted that the training was brief, and that she worked with her leadership team and former colleagues to better understand the Danielson model. She went on to explain that she took the parts of the training she liked and kept these, while alternating parts of how the evaluation system looked in practice.

For example, Ms. Cohen increased the frequency of the observations she conducted and allowed herself to weight certain parts of the overall evaluation more heavily, depending on what she felt was most important to the success of her students. Ms. Cohen said that she did not receive any formal feedback on how she was evaluating her teaching staff, and that her authorizer did make sure she was evaluating the teachers in her building, but did not provide her any specific feedback on the process.

Mr. Sherman worked in a traditional public school as a teacher for one year before getting his master's degree and principal certification. Mr. Sherman took over as the principal at his current school four years ago. His Charter Management Organization (CMO) provided the teacher evaluation system, which, like Ms. Cohen, he describes as a variation of the Danielson Framework. Mr. Sherman and his staff were also trained by a Danielson employee on how to use the system.

However, Mr. Sherman was quick to note that his CMO gave him some autonomy regarding how the Danielson Framework could look in practice. Mr. Sherman said he did not receive any formal feedback on how he was evaluating his staff. He noted that if there was a perceived issue his CMO might contact him, but as long as he was completing the evaluations, he did not receive any feedback on how he was navigating the evaluation process.

The two principals in this study worked in schools and contexts that were quite similar. Both Ms. Cohen and Mr. Sherman worked in the same large, urban area in Michigan. Both schools in this study were chartered by Michigan public universities. Ms. Cohen's school, which served grades K–6 and enrolled just over 300 students, had a free and reduced lunch eligibility rate of 98 percent. Mr. Sherman's school, which served grades K–7 and enrolled almost 650 students, had a free and reduced lunch percentage of 88 percent. Both Ms. Cohen's and Mr. Sherman's school served primarily African American students (81 percent and 94 percent, respectively).

While some demographic information for each school is similar, there are two important differences between these schools. First, Ms. Cohen's school is independently operated, while Mr. Sherman's school is operated by a CMO. Second, the schools' scores on the Michigan Accountability Scorecard are quite different. Ms. Cohen's school is currently labeled red, which is the lowest possible label on Michigan's Accountability Scorecard ranking, while Mr. Sherman's school is currently rated lime, which is the second highest possible state ranking (see table 3.1).

Data Analysis

All data were organized using ATLAS.ti software and analyzed to interpret patterns, trends, commonalities, and links among the participants (Miles & Huberman, 1994). Codes were developed inductively and, as themes emerged from the coding process, they were grouped together by theme (Miles & Huberman, 1994). All code groupings were then reviewed to find common excerpts that highlighted similar and different themes and ideas.

The final list of code groups are as follows:

1. Communication and feedback between principals and teachers
2. Data use, including how data was used in teacher evaluations and how principals used data to make decisions
3. Challenges experienced by principals while navigating these systems
4. Principal prior knowledge and experience, and how this impacts the way they think about and enact teacher evaluation systems

5. How relationships impact the way teacher evaluation systems are used
6. Teacher evaluation system specifics, including how this system was created, adopted, and modified, and the overall logistical processes of evaluating teachers

After completing this coding, the credibility of the coding process was checked by recoding the data for a second time. Any discrepancies were noted and addressed in order to refine and justify assertions and to look for possible alternative interpretations of the data (Miles & Huberman, 1994). Once the codes were identified, common stories, themes, and ideas were grouped together as similar data, generalizing within the case. After the coding process was complete, quotations were compared to original interview text, making sure they were taken in context. Groups of quotations were then put together as similarities and differences emerged.

Establishing Credibility

To establish credibility, participants were contacted to clarify any questions that arose during the transcribing and coding of the data. In qualitative research, there are several threats to credibility, including researcher bias, reactivity, and manipulation of the data (Miles & Huberman, 1994). These potential biases were addressed by ensuring all participants were allowed to read transcripts of recorded information and notes. All participants were given the opportunity to address any discrepancies that they felt did not accurately portray what they were trying to say or do. Additionally, critical feedback from colleagues was solicited throughout the data collection and writing process.

Limitations

There are several limitations to the design and methodology of this study. First, this study was limited by the two principals included in the work. The principals in this study shape the findings by their experiences, thoughts, actions, and beliefs. If data were collected from two other principals, the findings may look different. Second, although each principal was observed in their natural environment implementing their teacher evaluation system, the researcher did not observe each principal multiple times, with a variety of teachers, or during every interaction the principal had.

In this way, the data collected may not be a complete representation of everything the principals did while making sense of their teacher evaluation system. Finally, as with all qualitative research, it is important to acknowledge that the presence of the researcher may have impacted what was observed during data collection.

FINDINGS

This research sheds light onto how principal leadership is enacted in charter schools. The results show charter school principals experience flexibility and autonomy when implementing their school's teacher evaluation system. The principals used this flexibility to prioritize certain instructional goals for their schools. Additionally, because of this flexibility, the principals in this study were able to use their teacher evaluation systems as a means to work toward larger, local goals, including using teacher evaluations as a tool to train teachers to become mentors and as a tool to retain teachers.

Flexibility

The principals in this study stated that they experienced flexibility when implementing their teacher evaluation system. This flexibility resulted in these school leaders having autonomy when conducting teacher observations, when assigning weight and value to certain areas within the evaluation system (i.e., student assessment growth, professional development), and in how they used the results of teachers' evaluation data. Because of this flexibility, the principals in this study suggested they were able to tailor their individual teacher evaluation systems in a way they felt would most benefit their school, teachers, and students. Ms. Cohen said:

> I can adjust as needed. That's the beauty of a charter school. Curriculum, finance, facilities, your evaluation. When you are a charter and especially when you're an independent charter, you can see the deficit areas in your school, and you can address them right now. I don't have to wait to go through multiple channels to make a change. Being an independent charter, if you have a strong school leader and management team it is much better, because I can look at whatever I want. If I know that as a school we are struggling in reading, I can change my tool to put a heavier focus in the evaluation on the reading.

Ms. Cohen referred back to her time working in teacher and leadership roles in traditional public school settings, and noted that the systems she experienced in these settings were much more structured and difficult to adapt. As a result, even if the school principal thought some part of the evaluation system should be adjusted in an effort to improve instruction and student learning, this was often not possible, as principals were expected to follow the evaluation system as envisioned by district leaders. Ms. Cohen elaborated: "Working at a charter school, I have more flexibility. The buck stops here. I don't have to go to the district to do things I need to do to make this a better school."

Mr. Sherman also commented that he had the flexibility to adjust his school's evaluation system yearly, if needed. He took advantage of this flexibility by adjusting his school's teacher evaluation system to focus on areas where his school struggled in previous years. He said, "We evaluate (our teacher evaluation system) throughout the year. This year, we spent a little bit more time with data in evaluations. Data is a focus for us this year."

Mr. Sherman went on to comment that he and other members of his leadership team noticed student data was not a focus of the teachers in his building. Because both he and the leadership believed strongly in using student data to improve teaching, Mr. Sherman was able to emphasize using student data in his teacher evaluation system by requiring teachers to track, analyze, and share their student assessment data throughout the year, including during the evaluation process. Mr. Sherman was able to shift this instructional focus before the school year started in an effort to do what he thought would most improve teaching and learning.

In sum, the principals in this study experienced some degree of flexibility in using their school's teacher evaluation system. These results were corroborated in principal interviews, as well as principal observations and notes. For example, during the post-observation conference with her teacher, Ms. Cohen referred several times to the school's emphasis on reading instruction and student reading data.

The teacher acknowledged this, suggesting that this has been a focus for teachers throughout the school year. Additionally, Ms. Cohen chose to observe this teacher during a reading lesson, and the feedback she provided this teacher focused primarily on the teacher's reading instruction.

Ms. Cohen: A Tool for Creating Mentors

The flexibility experienced by the principals in this study during teacher evaluations provided them an opportunity to emphasize certain instructional areas during the evaluation process. Additionally, the flexibility afforded to these principals allowed them to use evaluations as tool to address the larger, local priorities of their school. For Ms. Cohen, one of her primary goals was to create mentors who would support the school into the future. Ms. Cohen used her teacher evaluation system as a way to support and train teachers to become mentors who shared her vision. She said:

> I have found that mentors are a huge component [to overall school success]. I have two lead teachers, one for K–2 and one for 3–6. They do not have any more experience than any others, but they are just naturals. They came in and they just know what to do. They know how to manage their class. I put them in a leadership role. I find that works really well, because sometimes teachers don't want to admit to their administrator that they're struggling, because they're afraid that it will count against them on their evaluation, which it does not. I don't work that way. Being able to have someone to go to is nice.

Ms. Cohen went on to explain that she felt satisfied that she was creating successful teacher mentors who were positively impacting her school. Ms. Cohen has found this type of teacher-to-teacher collaboration more effective at times than the feedback she gives teachers. Because of this, Ms. Cohen is constantly looking for her strongest teachers to take an active leadership role with her staff in an effort to collaborate with and improve instruction in her building.

During the observed teacher evaluation post-conference, much of the discussion between the teacher and Ms. Cohen focused on the teacher becoming a school mentor. They talked extensively about the teacher's future, including the work they would do together over the summer, the teachers they would target to support in the future, and any potential training or professional development that this teacher would like to attend to grow as a leader. In all, half of the post-conference focused on the teacher's observation and evaluation rating, and the other half focused on the teacher becoming a mentor and school leader into the future.

While Ms. Cohen said she has experienced positive results using teacher evaluations as a tool for creating mentors, she also mentioned this was not without challenges:

> It's not challenging to evaluate my teachers, but it's challenging to get them where they need to be. There's one me and I'm the most veteran person here. The challenge is trying to figure out how to coach these teachers quickly. When I was at my other school, we were a top performing school. Top of the charts. Had a lot of mentors in the building. Had a great mentor program. Most of my staff has less than three years' experience. I'm the first school that they've ever been to. They came straight out of college. The teacher you observed is in her fourth year, and she is the most veteran teacher in the building. I just started giving her mentoring responsibilities.

In sum, Ms. Cohen, whether it was during her interviews, during observations, or in the feedback and notes she provided her teacher, constantly stressed the importance of creating teacher mentors. Instead of the principal giving top-down instructions on how to best teach and improve learning, Ms. Cohen often let teachers mentor other teachers in an effort to improve instruction and work toward school goals.

These teachers were asked to extend the principal's vision of what effective teaching looked like to the goals of the school and principal. While challenging, Ms. Cohen confirmed that using teacher evaluations for this purpose was in the best interest of the future of her school.

Mr. Sherman: A Tool for Retaining Teachers

Mr. Sherman used the flexibility he was granted to focus on an instructional goal of teacher's tracking, understanding, and using student data. Beyond this, he too used this flexibility to work toward a larger, local goal for his school. In his case, Mr. Sherman used the flexibility he was afforded regarding his school's teacher evaluation system as a tool for retaining teachers. He referred back to the idea that it is often difficult for his school to retain quality teachers. Because of this Mr. Sherman used teacher evaluations as a way to provide positive and valuable feedback to his teachers, and provide those teachers with the resources necessary to make their job easier and improve their practice.

Mr. Sherman noted that, while his school does not have trouble finding teachers to hire, he does put an emphasis on hiring teachers who have a shared vision of his school and community. In his experience, these teachers will remain teaching at his school for the long term. Mr. Sherman said:

> We're good at getting teachers. Are we good at getting teachers who want to come for the right reasons? That's sometimes the issue or the challenge. People want jobs, so they're going to come here and talk well and speak the language and the lingo to get what they're trying to get, but sometimes those teachers are not working out. The right reason would be, understanding your surroundings and what you're walking into, and then being there with a purpose.

Mr. Sherman went on to say that teacher evaluations play a role in keeping the teachers he and other members of his leadership team want in their building:

> Evaluations are important. They're very powerful and they can help in keeping teachers, younger teachers. If I know I need a teacher who I want to be here for a while, it doesn't necessarily mean I'm going jack up her score. I'm going give him or her what he or she deserves, but at the same time, you need to use resources and make sure that relationship is built. You got to make sure that you show support to all your teachers, but especially those who make your job easier and the ones you want to keep. I mean, that's just normal, natural. If somebody's making something in your life easier, they need to know that they are important and that you want them around.

When asked specifically how teacher evaluations played into helping keep teachers in his building, Mr. Sherman said he provided detailed feedback to all the teachers, and provided them with things, from instructional resources to support from other teachers and administrators. Mr. Sherman was quick to point out that these things are necessary to improve teacher practice and become a better teacher, but are also essential for helping teachers feel supported and making his school a place where they want to remain teaching. He said:

> We differentiate instruction. When kids come to us, we don't just teach them the same thing all the way through. We have differentiated evaluations. I think there are some areas where you have to have a little wiggle room. If you have a teacher that, let's say, she's the bomb when it comes to parent relations. She's the bomb when it comes to her interaction with her students. The parents love her because she goes above and beyond. She's here after school. She's at all the games. She supports the school. I think there's some wiggle room there (to be flexible with a teacher's evaluation), because you see the attempt. You see the tenacity.

The support Mr. Sherman provided to his teaching staff was evident during the observation of his teacher. Before the lesson, he talked to the teacher about everything from life events to family, specifically asking what he could do to support this teacher both within school and outside of school. Mr. Sherman did not ask anything about the lesson, or what he would be observing. After the observation, he explained that he uses teacher evaluation systems to provide teachers with actionable and supportive feedback that will help teachers improve and feel comfortable and appreciated, not only in his school, but also outside of the school.

Mr. Sherman went on to say that providing this type of support and feedback throughout the teacher evaluation process is no guarantee that teachers will remain in his building. However, in his experience as an administrator, teachers often leave when they do not feel supported by administrators. Because of this, using the teacher evaluation system as a means to support teachers, especially his best teachers, is a priority at his school.

In sum, Mr. Sherman's primary goal in using teacher evaluations is to support teachers in an effort to retain these teachers. While using teacher evaluations as a means of support is not unique to the charter school landscape (Kraft & Gilmour, 2015), Mr. Sherman emphasized supporting teachers and retaining teachers much more frequently than using teacher evaluations as a means to rate teachers and dismiss teachers, two traditional ways to use teacher evaluations (Hanushek & Rivkin, 2010).

DISCUSSION

The two charter school principals in this study had flexibility when evaluating teachers in their respective buildings. This flexibility is consistent with previous research suggesting that charter school principals are typically granted greater latitude in the operation of their school than their traditional public school principal peers (Allen & Consoletti, 2010; Bickmore & Dowell, 2011; Dressler, 2001; Gawlik, 2008).

Additionally, the principals in this study constantly referred back to the idea of addressing local goals and priorities through using their school's teacher evaluation system. Ms. Cohen used her teacher evaluation system to create teacher mentors. This finding is consistent with prior research that suggests charter schools often use a distributed leadership approach, where principals work to grow their own leaders from the teachers they hire, train, and evaluate in their buildings (Louis et al., 2010; Merseth, 2009).

Mr. Sherman prioritized using his school's teacher evaluation system as a tool for teacher retention. This goal makes sense. given the research that suggests charter schools typically experience higher teacher turnover than traditional public schools (Miron & Applegate, 2007; Stuit & Smith, 2012) as well as research that suggests teachers improve their practice with experience and typically improve their practice as they remain in the same building for multiple years (Chetty et al., 2014; Rockoff, 2004). This goal also makes sense given past research showing that administrative support is one of the most important factors that impacts teacher retention decisions (Boyd, Grossman, Ing, Lankford, & Wyckoff, 2011; Leithwood et al., 2004).

Like traditional public school principals, the principals in this study are taking on the dual role of coach and evaluator (Duke & Stiggins, 1986, 1990) and are expected to be instructional leaders who are held accountable for student learning and school improvement (Blasé et al., 2010; Smylie, 2010). However, unlike their traditional public school peers, the participants in this study experienced less defined roles and expectations for what to emphasize during teacher evaluations and when using teacher evaluation information. As a result, these principals were able to make their own decisions, and tailor how their teacher evaluation systems look in practice.

The flexibility these principals employed when implementing teacher evaluation systems is a double-edged sword. First, because of this flexibility, principals were able to be nimble and react to local instructional needs, such as tailoring their evaluation systems to focus on reading or data use. Additionally, the principals were able to use teacher evaluations as a tool for focusing on larger, local priorities. Some research argues that policies should be able to be adapted to meet local needs (McLaughlin & Talbert, 1993), and giving local actors more say in how policies work in practice may in fact be a net positive for promoting teacher, student, and school growth.

However, the other edge of the sword is that principals in this study used this flexibility to address needs not central to the policy aims of teacher evaluation reform. In the state of Michigan and nationally, steps have been taken to better standardize the teacher evaluation process by calling for more clarity, accountability, and transparency in teacher evaluation systems (Hill & Grossman, 2013; U.S. Department of Education, 2009).

While not generalizable to all charter schools, the results of this work indicate that charter school principals use teacher evaluation systems to work toward local goals and priorities, and not necessarily toward the goals envisioned by policy makers. This is potentially worrisome, in the sense that it shows how a policy can be co-opted and used for reasons outside the scope of the policy design. While the principals in this study were acting in good faith and doing what they believed was in the best interest of their respective schools and students, the results indicate that there is a mismatch between policy makers' intentions and practitioners' implementation.

IMPLICATIONS FOR PRACTICE

This study has several implications for policy makers and practitioners, including principals in both charter schools and traditional public schools. First, given the amount of flexibility the principals in this study employed when implementing and tailoring teacher evaluation policies, it is imperative that these school leaders receive targeted training and professional development that supports the best use of these systems.

While the principals in this study each received some training on how to use the teacher evaluation systems, both principals described their training as incomplete, leaving themselves to make sense of and assign meaning to these systems. As a result, the principals in this study, at least in part, appear to be focusing on very specific aspects of a teacher's ability (focusing on their reading instruction or how they use student data), which raises a concern that these evaluations are undervaluing a teacher's overall performance.

The initial training of new teacher evaluation systems is a crucial element in how principals come to understand and implement these systems. All principals would likely benefit from more in-depth and detailed initial teacher evaluation training when adopting new teacher evaluation systems. In this way, principals may be more likely to use these systems in the way policy makers envisioned when adopting these systems. Policies may still be adapted to local contexts, but strengthening the initial training and support for principals has the potential to provide a more aligned vision between policy makers' intentions and practitioners' implementation efforts.

Second, all principals should receive specific feedback on how they are evaluating teachers, citing specifics about their evaluative process, not just that they are in compliance and completing what is required. This feedback should be extended to how principals are observing teachers, what they are using teacher evaluations for, and the overall process of evaluating teachers. This is increasingly becoming the case in traditional public school districts in an effort to work toward uniformity across districts and to reduce the subjectivity of teacher evaluations.

However, because charter schools do not have to worry about consistency of evaluations across a district and between schools, this training and feedback is often more limited in the charter school context. CMOs and charter authorizers would do well to provide increased training and explicit rationale to all charter school principals regarding the best use of teacher evaluation systems, including how to use these systems to help teachers improve their practice. Often this type of structured and detailed training is missing for many charter school principals and, as a result, they are forced to make sense of how to best use teacher evaluation systems on the fly and with little support.

Finally, because teacher evaluation policies do not operate in isolation, and principals make sense of these policies while making sense of outside factors, policy makers should consider these various interactions when designing future teacher evaluation systems. Policy makers and school leaders should work together and support the mutual efforts of discovering what makes a quality teacher and a quality teacher evaluation system.

If, in fact, charter school principals are experiencing success in retaining quality teachers by using resources associated with teacher evaluations (i.e., feedback and other supports), this would be useful information for policy makers to know. Additionally, if charter school principals are experiencing success in developing teacher mentors, which is strengthening their teaching staff, this is something else policy makers would do well to consider when designing future teacher evaluation policies.

CONCLUSION

Evaluating teachers is one of the most important and difficult responsibilities of school leaders. This research suggests that, unlike their traditional public school principal peers who are experiencing greater definition of their roles and expectations during teacher evaluations (Goldring et al., 2015), the charter school principals in this study have more flexibility to implement their teacher evaluation system based on what they believe is in the best interest of the school. Given the importance of teacher evaluations, researchers and practitioners must ensure that principals are using this flexibility in a way that actually improves teacher quality and, ultimately, student learning.

The flexibility these charter school principals used in regard to evaluation systems suggests that there is a greater chance for context to play a role in how these systems are used in practice. The principals in this study were doing what they believed was in the best interest of their school and, in fact, how they used these systems may have been beneficial for their teachers and students. However, the participants in this study used teacher evaluations for goals outside of the traditional understanding of how teacher evaluation policies should be used.

In short, contextual pressures led the charter school principals in this study to use teacher evaluation policies as a way to solve local problems, in this case creating teacher mentors and retaining teachers. This approach was not inherently bad, and may in fact have resulted in positive outcomes for these individual schools, but the results of this work speak to why consistent policy implementation, specifically teacher evaluation policy implementation, remains a challenge.

This study contributes to the literature that addresses how the charter school principal context impacts teacher evaluation system implementation. This study provides opportunities for future research on how charter school principals (and traditional public school principals) think about using teacher evaluations to build and grow a teaching staff.

For example, can teacher evaluations serve the dual purpose of providing useful feedback for teachers to help them improve their practice, while holding them accountable for their performance? And are principals, both in traditional public schools and charter schools, properly equipped to assist in achieving these goals? If not, what support and training can best support all principals to achieve these goals? As the importance of identifying high-quality teachers through teacher evaluations increases, so too must the research detailing how school leaders think about evaluating the teachers in their buildings.

Finally, this study highlights the emphasis charter school principals place on developing teacher leaders from within their community of teachers, and keeping these teachers in their buildings. Although the findings of the participants in this study cannot be generalized to charter school principals as a whole, they do provide some understanding of how charter school principals think about navigating the process of evaluating their teachers.

Chapter Four

Balancing Progressive Education and Performance Management

Erin Coghlan and Heinrich Mintrop

Student performance data, accountability for performance targets, teacher evaluations, and rewards and sanctions are ingredients of present teacher performance management systems in many jurisdictions, especially jurisdictions that serve low-income and disadvantaged populations. One such program, which blends together teacher evaluations, performance metrics, and financial bonuses into a single performance management program, is the Teacher Incentive Fund (TIF), a federal initiative launched in 2006 that has grown into a billion-dollar-plus program operating in 36 states (U.S. Department of Education, 2016).

In the fall of 2009, three public charter schools and a nonprofit organization that had been providing support to the schools applied for TIF funding. In return for the grant, recipients were expected to design a performance management system that followed broad federal guidelines. According to these guidelines, grantees were to measure teacher performance based on standardized student achievement test scores and, where possible, value-added measures. Teaching was to be evaluated in both a formative and summative way using rigorous evaluation instruments, and bonuses would be paid depending on a variety of indicators that summed up the teachers' measured effectiveness status.

The three schools in this study were stand-alone charter schools, not part of a charter network or management organization, and were founded as progressive alternatives to the regular district schools. All three schools served low-income minority students, with a social justice mission driving the school philosophy. Presumably, a good number of the teachers were attracted to the schools because they encouraged a critical and progressive pedagogy, a constructivist teaching orientation, and a mission of social justice and ameliorating societal inequalities.

CHARTER SCHOOLS AS (PERHAPS) CONDUCIVE ENVIRONMENTS FOR PERFORMANCE MANAGEMENT

Public-sector institutional contexts, such as public school districts, have shown resistance to management reforms along private sector lines (Trujillo, 2013). Unions have been known to defend single salary scales (Podgursky, 2006), rules governing teacher tenure may stand in the way of teachers being responsive to evaluations (Millman & Darling-Hammond, 1990), and administrators may shy away from potential conflict that arises from teachers' micro-political disputes (Timperley & Robinson, 1998).

Teachers in the charter schools we study were non-tenured, non-unionized, and were paid on a salary schedule that allowed for differential pay beyond seniority. Annual contract renewal depended on performance, and was at the discretion of school administrators and governing boards. As independent non-networked schools, the charter schools experienced the full weight of the state's accountability system, and were also exposed to market competition with traditional public schools and other charters. Thus, unlike typical public schools, the three charter schools in this study existed in a relatively deregulated space, commonly thought to be conducive for performance management.

Despite these conditions, on the face of it, the schools were perhaps unlikely candidates for a TIF grant. All three schools embraced culturally relevant curriculum and teaching practices, a personalized learning climate for students, and an appreciation for self-determined professional learning. A performance management system emphasizing goals, measurement, rewards, and careful monitoring seemed out of place in—or at the very least in tension with—such an environment. Yet, as we will see, the school leaders saw their schools as both progressive and performance-oriented and, if anything, were intrigued by the management approach of TIF.

Leaders took on the program in 2010–2011 for a duration of five years. During this time, disappointments and tensions arose that leaders tried to attenuate. With the help of 29 interviews and 2 focus groups, we show how leaders negotiated the situation, how they stepped forward, retreated and, in the end, made the best of the situation.

While the TIF performance management system was comprehensive, we focus primarily on one aspect—teaching evaluations—for the simple fact that this element of the system proved to have the longest stamina and potential to influence school culture. Important lessons can be learned from the efforts of these charter school leaders, and are discussed at the conclusion of the chapter.

About TIF in the Three Schools

The Teacher Incentive Fund was initially funded by the federal government as a way to improve teaching practices, to reform evaluation and compensation for both teachers and principals, and to attract and retain effective teachers in low-income, hard-to-staff schools (U.S. Department of Education, 2016). As mentioned, grant recipients were offered the flexibility to design a program that best suited their unique needs, as long as the program awarded financial bonuses based on value-added measures, student academic achievement on standardized tests, and teacher evaluations.

The schools in this study chose to design a system that primarily awarded financial bonuses to teachers based on school-wide goals such as graduation and college matriculation rates; student outcomes on several state standardized tests that were linked to individual teachers in the two core subjects, English and mathematics, via value-added scores; and performance on both formative and summative evaluations. The exact amount that teachers could earn from the bonus varied depending on the subject area and grade level taught, but on average, teachers could earn a maximum of $10,500.

The direct recipients of the TIF grant were the three charter schools, but a nonprofit organization (hereafter referred to as the "provider") providing teacher and instructional leadership support was responsible for grant monitoring and capacity building. The provider had a previous working relationship with each of the school leaders, and the principals at the schools contributed to the TIF grant application. Once the grant was received, researchers at University of California, Berkeley (including the authors of this chapter) were contracted by the nonprofit to evaluate the program.

The school leaders worked with the provider to create a performance management system that included formative and summative evaluation components. Principals or instructional leaders committed to monthly formative classroom observations for all teachers, which would result in a holistic "formative evaluation of teaching" (FET) score. During observations, leaders used a rubric that was designed using select elements from the California Standards for the Teaching Profession (California Commission on Teacher Credentialing, 2009).

For the "summative evaluation of teaching" (SET), participation was voluntary. Those that chose to participate would submit a video of their best example of a lesson in the spring of each year. The video was externally scored by the provider organization, which trained raters with expertise in teacher professional development to score and provide feedback to the submitted lessons using an observation and feedback instrument (the SET).

The SET, which was loosely based on the Danielson Framework of Teaching (Danielson, 2007), was used by the external raters to evaluate teachers on the degree to which their lessons activated prior knowledge, generated curiosity, provided clear explanations, co-constructed knowledge, checked for student understanding, enabled students to gradually do independent work, and built on student ideas and misconceptions in giving feedback.

Teachers were initially trained by school leaders about how to use the SET instrument during the first year of implementation. They had access to the SET rubric throughout the year. Designers of the management system expected teachers to use the tool to help guide their planning, and to inform collaborative learning in discipline-oriented inquiry groups or other teacher team meetings. In addition, school leaders contracted with an outside organization to design an online data dashboard. The dashboard was intended to give teachers immediate and ongoing access to the breakdown of their bonus award and to the variety of performance indicators.

LITERATURE REVIEW

Evaluations of TIF programs across the United States tell us that intricate performance management systems are replete with technical and social complexities that lead to enormous implementation challenges at both district and school levels (Rice et al., 2012). Creating reliable value-added measures, implementing new technology and data processing streams, and integrating new performance measures into the organizational environment have been found to constrain the capacity of schools and districts (Malen et al., 2015; Marsh et al., 2011; Max et al., 2014; Milanowski, Witham, Schuermann, Kimball & Pietryka, 2010; Rice et al., 2012).

Likewise, dispositions, at least in traditional public schools, may be adverse to payment for performance and evaluations, which may attribute to implementation complications. As mentioned, unions often do not support the idea (Podgursky, 2006), and traditional egalitarian norms (Marsh et al., 2011), uniform salary scales based on seniority (Podgursky, 2006), and tenure (Millman & Darling-Hammond, 1990) may mitigate against acceptance of salary differentials and performance competition. All these features were not present in the three charter schools we studied. Teachers in the charters were used to differential pay, they had no tenure, and were let go if they showed low performance.

Teacher evaluations, the one component of the performance management system that we focus on, pose a specific challenge. In education, evaluations typically serve two main purposes: they can provide informal or formative feedback for learning and improvement to meet a desired goal or standard

(Black & Wiliam, 1998; Taras, 2005), or they can provide a more conclusive summative judgment of performance based on given criteria (Taras, 2005).

In the case of formative evaluations in schools, school principals or instructional leaders typically will use formative assessments to observe classrooms and give ongoing, non-punitive feedback to teachers to improve learning and instruction over time (Black & Wiliam, 1998). School leaders use summative evaluations, on the other hand, to make conclusive judgments about the performance of teachers (Popham, 1988). Summative evaluations may be used to determine consequences, such as the terms of teacher employment (Murphy, Hallinger, & Heck, 2013).

In a performance management system like TIF, both the summative and formative functions of evaluation are linked to the financial bonus. In a logic of expectancy, teachers are likely to give value to the summative aspect of evaluations if they believe they can improve their performance and can maximize their bonus award through their effort (Podgursky & Springer, 2007) or if they can improve in their status as high performers (Buunk & Gibbons, 2007).

In a more formative logic, teachers may embrace evaluations if they consider the evaluative criteria as reflective of their own teaching style (Clandinin, Kennedy, Rocque, & Pearce, 1996; Kimball, 2002), and if they desire to learn how to become better teachers and see the evaluation rubric as a guiding tool in this endeavor (Danielson & McGreal, 2000). However, summative and formative aspects of evaluation may often be in tension with each other (Harlen & James, 1997).

How the integration of formative and summative evaluations plays out at a school may depend, in large part, on the climate of organizational learning in the school. We infer from the research literature that a climate of trust, supportive leadership, and an emphasis on professional learning may increase the likelihood that formative and summative purposes of evaluations may be integrated (Darling-Hammond, Wise, & Pease, 1983; Danielson, 2011; Davis, Ellett, & Annunziata, 2002; Pianta & Hambre, 2009). Strong instructional leaders may offer precise feedback, address learning needs at various levels of teacher performance, and create a professional development climate that fosters teacher learning.

Unfortunately, these environments are not the norm. Literature on instructional leadership indicates that leaders for the most part tend to provide trivial, non-specific feedback that is not always delivered in a timely way (Darling-Hammond, 2013; Milanowski & Heneman, 2001). Nor have instructional leaders been willing to make high-stakes decisions based on evaluations (Darling-Hammond et al., 1983; Hallinger, Heck, & Murphy, 2014; Tucker, 1997). Instead, it is more likely that administrators treat evaluations as more of a compliance task (Hallinger et al., 2014).

What distinguishes the three stand-alone charters from other environments for evaluation may be that they, with the help of the provider, were able to design evaluation criteria and instruments as they saw fit. And they opted for a relatively simple tool that picked up on features of basically effective lessons.

METHODOLOGY

The methodology of this study uses a qualitative, multiple case study research design (Creswell, 2014; Yin, 2009). This approach is commonly used to study social policies, including policy innovations in education (Yin, 2009). A total of 29 semi-structured interviews were conducted over three time periods.

The first round of interviews occurred in academic year 2010–2011, during the planning year of the program. The second round was in academic year 2012–2013 during the second implementation year, and the last interview round was in the third implementation year, academic year 2013–2014. Two focus groups were held in the final implementation year of 2014–2015. All principals, instructional leaders, and coaches at each school were interviewed at least once, and leaders of the provider organization were interviewed at least once as well. In some cases we asked leaders, especially toward the end of the program, to give retrospective accounts of their experiences and perceptions.

Analysis codes for interviews were developed using a theory-driven approach (Miles, Huberman, & Saldaña, 2014). The interviews were coded using Dedoose, a qualitative data analysis software. Drawing from literature on evaluations, financial incentives, teacher learning, and pedagogy, we developed 27 distinct codes. Some additional codes captured emergent phenomena.

The theory-derived codes were defined, operationalized, and illustrated with representative quotes from interviews before coding began. We then trained a team of four coders for inter-rater reliability. Two coders coded 20 percent of interview excerpts, and the discrepancies were identified and discussed among the coders to clarify concepts. After all interviews were coded, we created data matrices and reflection memos to analyze the findings. Table 4.1 presents examples of interview concepts, dimensions, and questions.

FINDINGS

The findings are organized around four sections that are roughly chronological, but emphasize different aspects that were salient in distinct periods. In the first section, findings reveal the initial hopes of school leaders for the

Table 4.1. Interview Protocol Examples

Concepts	Sample Dimension	Sample Interview Questions
Goals	Benchmarks for improvement	For this school year, what goals have you emphasized or pursued to make the school better? Which goals have come from outside the school, and which are from inside? Would you say that teachers you work with share the same goals?
Learning culture	How leaders foster the adult learning culture	How would you describe the adult learning climate around instruction at your school? How do you conceptualize instructional expertise?
Performance management system fit	Gauging whether the performance management system fits into the school organization	As you know, TIF was supposed to be a performance management system that evaluates and rewards teachers differentially, and intends to improve the precision of feedback on teacher performance. What do you think about this idea now that you have participated?
Tools, instruments, feedback (FET)	Precision of diagnostics and feedback using the FET	One component of the TIF project was the FET for which you had to give a score for teachers. How did that play out for you? What do you mainly look at when you observe teachers? How do you communicate to teachers what your standards of instructional quality are?

Concepts	Sample Dimension	Sample Interview Questions
Tools, instruments, feedback (SET)	Precision of diagnostics and feedback using the SET	What did you think about the SET and the feedback that was provided to teachers? How do you ensure that the teachers apply standards of instructional quality to their own teaching?
Learning strategies	What strategies leaders use to facilitate instructional improvements	In order to facilitate improvements in instruction, what main strategies have you chosen for this year? Were these strategies chosen by the school or did you choose them?
Formative vs. summative	How leaders deal with tension between formative and summative evaluations	Do you encounter the tension between formative and summative evaluation in your work? How do you deal with it?
Future of TIF	What happens after the program ends	When you think about the end of TIF and the next generation of your evaluation and/or compensation system, what do you take away from TIF? What do you leave behind?

performance management system. In the subsequent sections, implementation issues came to the fore that merged with a realization of the negative repercussion of summative evaluations, which led to the ejection of the management approach. In the last section, we show how school leaders discarded elements of the system, but made a concerted effort to turn the evaluation component around and use it for valued ends. Pseudonyms are used for the three schools: Acorn, Bridge, and Cypress.

Beginnings: School Leaders See Seamless Connection between the Performance Management System and School Culture

When school leaders initially took on the TIF project, none of the schools had direct experience with performance management systems, but the TIF program requirements seemed normatively unproblematic. School leaders saw their schools as innovative and pathbreaking. They were familiar with conditions of competition, external scrutiny, and public visibility. Using differential pay, evaluations, and increased focus on student achievement data and school-wide performance metrics were not initially off-putting to the school leaders.

During interviews, school leaders were excited about the opportunity to join the TIF program and were particularly motivated by the prospect of garnering additional resources to help offset financial imbalances at the schools, and to increase teacher salaries. Schools had received TIF funding in 2010, just two years after the financial crisis hit the U.S. economy, and during a time when the state was slashing its education budget in order to help offset deficits. As noted by a provider organization leader, who originally applied for the grant:

> It was a win/win. Because we had more money for professional development, more money for the schools, and money on top of salary. All of that was good. . . . What happened was the whole financial crisis and all the budget woes of the state, so the state was cutting right when we were implementing. So, the administrative costs—it really saved the positions, the principals' positions . . . the timing was perfect. Just putting extra money in operations was a challenge for our school during that time. As a charter school, the cash flow alone was an issue.

School leaders did not shy away from the technical requirements of the program; they imagined that the data dashboard, the increased use of student performance data, and the management of school-wide goals would be a boon to their organization. Leaders thought that increased use of data could provide schools with quantitative precision that would help them bring more awareness to student performance and organizational goals.

This was especially the case for the use of videos and evaluation rubrics that were quantitatively scored by external evaluators. Leaders hoped that the summative scores and comments from external evaluators could be used to provide additional feedback to teachers, who could work with instructional coaches to improve their practice. They wanted to develop shared understandings of what good teaching looked like, common expectations for students, and a systematic way to reward good teaching. As noted by an instructional leader at Cypress:

> My goals for the evaluation system, or what I hope their goal is, is sort of twofold. One is to streamline what we think a Cypress teacher is and what Cypress practices are. This is our tenth year. We have to be able to say to new staff, here's what Cypress teachers do. Here's what we're looking for. At least when I started, we weren't really able to do that. Or the things that we said we did weren't real. Or they were dreams we had for the future instead of what we're actually doing . . . We want to talk about, what are the Cypress sort of

ways—I mean, we'll find a better way to call that. And if we wanted to replicate them, what are the things that go into that? And I think the second goal of the evaluation should be consistency of practice. And by that, I don't mean that every teacher should be teaching the same way, because that's crazy. But instead, that we're meeting some sort of expectation; that all students are engaged; that our content is rigorous. That it's all inquiry-based instruction to meet these categories of things that people are evaluated on. Right now, I don't think its super consistent. And I think everybody can have an off day, myself included. But I think overall, we have to say, here's what we're looking for as a school.

Rewarding teachers with differential pay was not at odds with this agenda.

Program Implementation: Technical Difficulties amidst Organizational Change

Despite the initial excitement and hopes for TIF, the implementation of the performance management system turned out to be thorny. At the leadership level, attention to the TIF program early on had been directed towards the technical implementation of the program, such as establishing the reward algorithm and focusing on data flows and reporting. While the leaders took time to introduce teachers to the SET instrument, leaders paid less attention to orienting teachers toward other aspects of the performance management system, such as explaining how all of the performance metrics worked, or explaining how the bonuses would be computed. As described by the head of schools at Cypress: "We created something really complicated and nobody knows how it works. Well, they know how it works, but they don't know what the theory of action is, so it gets them a little bit less to invest in it, and to see it as just something that the school does, but it's not really driving their practice, which is an overall fail."

School leaders admitted that they did not have the capacity to take on the complexity of the program. When they originally received the grant, money had been set aside for a new position to take on the management of the program at each school. There were several managerial functions for the job, including collecting and reporting student and school-wide data, managing the rollout of the program, and ensuring instructional improvement was taking place with the performance management system.

Since resources were scarce, school leaders opted to take on the program management themselves and used the allocated resources elsewhere (either to purchase new technology for students, to backfill school operating costs, or to fill other positions). But the administrative teams in the schools were already stretched thin. As noted by the director of the provider organization:

> So, apparently in the proposal when they were negotiating who was going to do what, the school leaders said, "Oh, well if you just give us those extra

dollars, we'll do the data. I mean, we don't need to get a data person, what do we need that for?" They were thinking, "Oh, it's extra dollars in our budget." . . . So, I think what happened was . . . when they first signed on they said, "Yeah, we'll take the dollars and we'll do the data collection, blah blah blah." I don't think they completely understood what they were signing up for. So they, I think, thought it was going to be easier than it was. So what happened was, when it actually, when the complexity of all that was involved happened, they had already spent that money.

On the technical side, an organization had been contracted to provide an online data dashboard interface that would give teachers a breakdown of their bonus, including information on their value-added scores, school-wide performance data, and feedback from their summative evaluation. The contracted organization was unable to provide this service during the first two years of the project. As a result, teachers were not able to easily access the indicators that would show them how their bonus was constructed, nor were they able to receive the much-desired feedback on their SET submission.

While the TIF program was experiencing implementation challenges, the schools themselves were undergoing their own organizational changes. When Acorn and Bridge began implementing the program, they had new principals, both former teachers in their first year of leadership. They were both unfamiliar with the program requirements and had not collaborated on the original design of the evaluation instruments, nor had they participated in the original TIF grant application.

Bridge was also experiencing unique growing pains, since the school took in many new students during 2013 due to a school closure in the area. In light of its increased enrollment, Bridge decided to change locations for more space in the 2013–2014 school year, causing major disruptions to the daily routines of teachers and students.

Cypress was also growing at a rapid rate, and needed an entirely new organizational structure that would better support instructional leadership. In 2013, the school put into place three principals at each level of the K–12 school (elementary, middle, and high school), and then supported these new leaders with instructional coaches and case managers at each school level. The former school principal who had collaborated on the TIF grant application became the director of schools, and was no longer involved with the daily instructional practices of teachers.

During 2013, the state of California gave all schools a two-year reprieve from the testing requirements associated with the Annual Performance Index, in order to give schools time and resources to transition to the newly adopted Common Core State Standards. With that, the linchpin of bonus calculations vanished from the system, leaving only the scores for teaching evaluations and internal assessments in place as measures that had at least some legitimacy.

The Evaluation System Clashes with School Culture

Amidst these technical and organizational challenges, formative and summative evaluations began to lose traction in the schools. After the first SET scores were returned to the schools, several of the more senior teachers who envisioned themselves as high-status teachers did not score high enough to receive the bonus. As noted by the principal of Bridge:

> I think [a Bridge teacher] really freaked out over her SET score, which was a 2. Her FET score was a 3 and her SET score was a 2 and she was freaking out about the SET and just took it really personal that "I'm not a good teacher anymore and what does this mean." And then she had to think about it; [the score] just added stress that's de-motivating.

Moreover, the teachers received the SET feedback very late in the fall semester in the new school year, after they had already received their SET bonus months earlier. Teachers felt that receiving the feedback on the SET this late was not useful to their practice or to their ability to serve students better. Also, in some cases, external raters left the feedback boxes for the scores empty. Without thorough feedback, teachers were left with simple scores to interpret their results. An instructional leader at Cypress captures the disillusionment of the SET well:

> The SET . . . hasn't changed our instructional practices. I have some pretty specific reasons for that. One is, we just do it at the end of the year, and we never see it again. And so it doesn't help us think in the craft of teaching, where are the areas and indicators that I can use to get that? . . . The second reason it hasn't been helpful is I got my SET results from last year two weeks ago. And I—not just me—and so what—I got my bonus, like months ago, which is great. But I got the results, and the results don't tell me, like, anything about my instructional moves, right? . . . If the results don't coordinate to the video, if there's no narrative or even a checkbox of feedback, that stuff doesn't exist, so I can't use that to become a better teacher, and I don't think other people can either. That's what people have reflected. This is something I have to do. It doesn't make me a better teacher. If it did, I think Cypress would totally be behind it. Because our teachers are very growth-minded. We want to be better teachers for our students.

This disenchantment was shared throughout each of the schools, and leaders reported that teachers came to see the performance system as perfunctory. Because the evaluations failed to meld with teachers' expectations for the award and their professional learning norms in terms of feedback and strategies for improvement, much of the evaluation system fell to the wayside in the minds of teachers. Over time, several teachers submitted the SET because they saw it as a programmatic obligation and figured it was the only way to bump up their bonus award. As noted by the principal at Bridge:

> I think that generally people are kind of, like, it's something we have to do because we're getting this extra money. And it's great that we're getting this extra money . . . but I don't know how much it's really improving their teaching; that the SET just feels like something they have to do and not like an opportunity to show my best work. It's like, okay, I've got to do this and there's little pressure. . . . It's something I have to do to get that piece of the bonus. It's not really fully integrated into the culture.

In response to the backlash to the SET and the performance management system more broadly, leaders took a very hands-off approach during this phase, and let the program fall to the periphery of organizational life. During this time, leaders acknowledged that there was a mismatch between the evaluation system and the existing school culture, and that it became a "compliance piece" rather than a tool for deeper learning. As noted by the head of schools at Cypress:

> On SET, I think there's so much there that we're missing, that I think if we can build that into the "Cypress School Way" somehow . . . we totally fumbled that one. It was something that we could have done really well, and it was out the gate late, so we couldn't message it to teachers in a good way, and then it turned into a compliance task as opposed to a development task, and that always hurts things. Whenever we turn things into compliance tasks, we get low quality.

The formative evaluations did not fare much better. Leaders initially reported that the routines established with the more precise SET tool were useful for their own practice. Leaders felt that at the beginning, the monthly observation requirement helped them to give structure to their observation routines and provided a framework for giving feedback to teachers. As noted by the principal at Acorn:

> Well, for me the first year of this project was also the year that I became principal, and I became principal, like, by surprise and without any preparation. And so for me personally, the biggest thing that this accomplished was, it told me what to do. It was, like, you need to go observe nine times. Okay. You need to coach them to SET. So it just gave me instructions about what to do. These are assessments you need to give your students. Okay. Because I had no idea really what I was doing, and so I feel that, even though in the beginning I had a really hard time doing the things that it said to do because I was just so overwhelmed with so many other things with the job, I feel like it really gave

me a lot of guidance as to what you're supposed to do as an instructional leader at this school.

However, in the midst of the backlash against the summative component of the evaluations, the leaders abandoned their original commitment to use the SET criteria for formative conferences and reverted back to conducting formative evaluations in a more haphazard way. This avoided conflict with teachers, but left them frustrated as well:

> And so I feel like the FET is kind of—doesn't really . . . it's all, like, on the teacher, right. So it's like, does the teacher use multiple forms of assessment? Well, yeah, but it still doesn't help their kids learn any better, right. Or does the teacher plan alliance units? Well, yeah, but their delivery isn't good, so the kids still aren't getting it. So there are things where I feel like, teachers could check a lot of boxes on the FET and still not really be doing a good job of increasing student learning.

Efforts at Turnaround: Leaders Turn the SET into a Formative Tool

The spring of 2014 was a marker of transformations for the TIF program. During professional development sessions for school leaders with the provider in late fall 2013, the provider became more involved in giving feedback to school leaders by showing them the SET videos that had been submitted by their teachers. This reorientation was in part due to the provider organization's new director, who came into the role with a strong focus on instructional improvement and wanted to help school leaders salvage the professional development benefits of the formative component of the evaluations.

Having the video evidence in front of them, leaders developed problem awareness in new ways and began to see the utility of the SET tool for identifying components of effective classroom instruction. With this new lens, leaders began to reorient the use of the SET tool. They first began to downplay the bonus associated with the SET. In fact, leaders admitted that they actively avoided and discouraged public conversations about bonuses and data dashboards. Then they took the SET instrument and redesigned it to meet their professional development needs. By disentangling the instrument from the formal SET submission, the leaders redefined the SET tool as a learning resource for teachers, rather than a compliance task necessary to earn the bonus.

For example, Acorn reformatted the instrument to provide space for personal reflections, deleting spaces after each indicator for specific evaluative scores and feedback. This aesthetic modification helped teachers disassociate the summative purposes of the SET from the purpose of using the tool for everyday practice.

At Cypress, leaders recognized that the orientation of the SET tool toward basic teaching functions akin to a five-part lesson plan constrained the more organic, constructivist orientation preferred by some of their more senior teachers. In order for teachers to accept the tool, the leaders revised the tool to include more exploratory instructional formats. However, Bridge did not adopt the modified instrument created by Cypress, opting for the original emphasis on basic teaching functions.

The SET tool appeared in professional development sessions regularly conducted by the schools, less so in Cypress, more so in the other two schools. Acorn leaders, for example, used their version of the tool to guide the practice of filming lessons and lesson study into their collaborative learning groups. Leaders at Acorn also began again to use the SET tool for formative conferences. When reflecting on the TIF grant during the last round of interviews, the principal at Acorn recognized that more structure had been given to instructional lessons and student learning over time:

> And what I saw year after year in observations of teachers is that lessons didn't really have alignment. The teacher was just kind of talking, and what were the kids really doing? It just seemed like there was more vision around curriculum and assessments and projects but not on the daily, like, what's supposed to happen in your class. And so, kids were getting really inconsistent experiences. And I think that that's still somewhat true, but I think it's become way more consistent in the sense that teachers are trying to model and are trying to give independent practice time and trying to really think of what's a realistic objective for any given day.

Bridge also benefited from the changes they made in the last phase of the project. Like Acorn, Bridge also established the practice of lesson study, during which teachers would observe one another's classrooms or would sometimes film lessons, and then bring the videos back to professional development sessions for discussion. Bridge was the most successful at integrating the SET into collaborative inquiry groups and used the tool to frame group discussions. As noted by the principal at Bridge:

> The collaborative inquiry group that we started was all based around the SET last year. And it was based on looking at each component of a five-part lesson plan. So in some ways, they did get bought into it, and that wasn't my idea, I don't think, solely, definitively it wasn't my idea; it was a collaborative thing. And then this year, that morphed into—we actually started doing the same thing again and then we realized, that doesn't make sense. So then toward the middle of the year, what was kind of cool within it, everyone was breaking out based on what they wanted to learn and grow in. And then those became, like, three mini-groups.

At Bridge, the SET approach made a cautious comeback as a summative tool. When asked about her reflections on SET during the last year of the program, this is what the principal at Bridge had to say:

> I think we have pretty high implementation on SET, like, everyone's doing it and trying because it's part of their job. They're not just blowing it off. Everyone's doing it. So, the fact that some of the teachers who really thought they were doing really well, and I wasn't seeing that, and then I had the SET that also verified their performance, it kind of helped me—it just helped me in my supervision and trying to figure out who's a fit here and who's not, and also having that third point of information.

At Cypress, the "new" tool had mixed uptake. Leaders reported that some teachers approved of the modifications made to the SET instrument, but it was not fully embraced by all teachers, especially veteran teachers. However, instructional coaches found that the revised instrument was useful for helping to train new teachers, and the tool was also integrated into some collaborative inquiry group meetings at the school. As noted by an instructional coach at Cypress, "I think there's a lot of excitement around the new version of the SET tool that has a constructive lens. And then for my more beginning teachers, the five-part lesson is really a great teaching tool and guidance tool for them, as they're just learning about lesson design and instruction."

DISCUSSION

The prevailing commonsense logic within some education policy-making circles today is that reforms such as pay-for-performance and teacher evaluations are persuasive policy tools to improve the performance of schools. This is evident by the federal government's ongoing support of TIF, which to date has funded TIF grants operating in over 2,000 schools (U.S. Department of Education, 2016), and is sustained in the new Every Student Succeeds Act.

Charter schools, such as those in this study, may be more comfortable with programs that allow them to innovate with trending programs. They may be especially attuned to performance management of the TIF-inspired type, since charter schools are often familiar with deregulated labor-management relationships, differential pay, and hire-and-fire norms based on performance.

The three charter schools we studied were special cases, and exemplified hybrids of charter management principles, since they embraced both self-determined professionalism and student-centered progressivism. Clearly not all charter schools are such hybrids, but many charter schools seem to combine an avowed equity focus with private-sector type management principles. Thus far, our three cases may not be completely atypical for the field.

We were interested to see what leaders—especially the administrative team and instructional supervisors—in these three schools would do once they adopted TIF. How would they cope with the tension? Would they use their autonomy to tailor the system to their own ends? Would they find a way to avoid the typical TIF-related implementation challenges? Would they integrate formative and summative purposes of evaluation so that there was harmony between the purpose of learning and the purpose of rewarding performance?

We saw, in a nutshell, that the leaders were not able to forge such synthesis. They were able to bend the system to their own ends, but their ends shifted as well. In the beginning, they thought that the system would answer to many different needs: additional resources for their schools in times of economic cuts, data-based decision making, precision in performance evaluation, teacher learning around instruction, and rewarding the best teachers with bonuses that might compel them to firm up their commitments.

When faced with conflicts between the adopted management system and the strong negative sentiments, particularly for senior teachers, the school leadership did what one would predict from the literature: they opted for harmony, abandoned the high-stakes nature of the TIF approach, disregarded the summative evaluation tool, and decoupled formative learning from summative evaluations. Throughout they made sure that sufficient compliance was produced so that the TIF monies kept flowing. This was made easier because the whole TIF architecture was in disarray after the state had abandoned the student achievement assessments that were the linchpin of the whole approach.

Acting with ample autonomy, the charter school leaders could easily push most of the features of the performance management system to the periphery of organizational life when the system was not working as intended. Several of the data-reporting requirements still continued, and schools continued to receive funding, but leaders could undermine their own evaluative intent when the conditions seemed inauspicious.

This pattern of schools selectively buffering themselves from external programmatic demands is well documented in literature on internal coherence (e.g., Honig & Hatch, 2004), but what is interesting here is the extent to which the charter school leaders were able to flexibly change the program midstream in an organic, almost imperceptible way. The summative and incentive aspects of the evaluations, for example, fell by the wayside almost silently.

While the implementation of the program was far from perfect, the study clearly shows that the logic of performance management was not an easy fit for the progressive learning culture of the schools. The leaders in all three schools treasured the culture of collegial relationships and collegial learning over the performance management (while not letting go of the money). It was not so much egalitarianism or resistance to differential pay for differential performance that drove out performance management of the TIF type, but the inability of the system to prod and reinforce powerful learning around instruction. This inability had more to do with the technical deficiencies of the evaluation system, and less to do with normative discontinuities.

Aspects of the system were rescued when the leaders developed problem awareness about instructional quality that their schools demonstrated in the submitted videos. And when leaders were taught how to analyze these videos with the evaluation tool that they themselves had adopted, they wanted to make their new insights and learning fruitful for their faculties. Nothing hindered them from taking the tool and tailoring it to their local needs, then reintroducing it into faculty professional development.

Implementation capacity and conflict aversion are themes that are well known in the literature on evaluation and pay-for-performance, and that seems to apply to schools across the board. The charters studied here are no exception. But autonomy, adherence to an internal school culture in the face of the wrong external "medicine," and tinkering according to recognized needs when they arise are especially salient themes in the accounts from the three stand-alone charter schools.

As to the tension between performance management and progressivism, it would be too much to say that the schools' philosophical and cultural commitments to professional self-determination and progressivism were antithetical to performance management. Elements of performance management coexisted with these commitments prior to the advent of the TIF system, and continued throughout. But the TIF system brought the tension to a breaking point at which leaders had to make a decision in one way or another. It is to the credit of leaders in the three schools and the provider that they protected what they considered to be their cultural core, while finding ways to make elements of the management system fruitful for learning.

IMPLICATIONS FOR PRACTICE

The qualitative and longitudinal nature of this study allows for a closer view of a complex picture that reveals how charter school leaders tried to integrate an intricate and highly complex performance management system into the culture of their schools over time. Below are a few takeaway lessons for charter school leaders who are considering implementing a similar program.

Simple is better. Highly intricate performance data dashboards might seem to be an attractive tool, but this study, like many other studies in the research literature, show that these in all likelihood overtax the implementation capacity of even highly entrepreneurial schools. Instead, less is more.

School culture and internal coherence are treasures to be protected. The glue that held these three charter schools together was a unique learning culture that leaders did not dare to disrupt or enfeeble. Inconsistencies within this learning culture can be tolerated up to a specific point, but beyond this point, leaders need to act and selectively buffer and embrace program or system features.

Autonomy can be a powerful resource for leaders. In each phase of program implementation, the leaders in the three schools were able to tinker, adapt and, in the end, craft an approach that answered to the needs and valued ends in their faculties.

Summative purposes of evaluations must be fused with formative ones. Teachers in the three schools were not averse to the performance management system as long as they expected to benefit from it both cognitively and materially. It was only when the two functions clearly fell apart that the whole system was rejected. When this occurred, it was easier for leaders to sacrifice the summative and incentive function than let go of the quest for formative learning. In the case of the three charter schools, meaningfulness for teacher learning turned out to be a more powerful motive for teachers' acceptance of evaluations than rewarding good performance.

Chapter Five

Principalship Succession and Socialization in Charter Schools

Marytza A. Gawlik

Charter schools are under tremendous pressure to demonstrate higher levels of student achievement than traditional public schools in order to garner legitimacy (Hannan & Freeman, 1984), compete for students, and satisfy accountability requirements. The literature on traditional schools has shown that the principalship has an important influence on school success (Boris-Schacter & Langer, 2002; Cambron-McCabe & McCarthy, 2005; Hoy & Miskel, 2008).

Specifically, strong and stable principals, sufficient time to build relationships with staff, the empowerment of key parties, and visionary thinking are essential to academic success (Hoy & Miskel, 2008). The pivotal role of school principalship (Berman & McLaughlin, 1978; Datnow, Hubbard, & Mehan, 2002) is intensified in charter schools, in part because these organizations are often (though not always) inspired and developed by a small group of individuals.[1]

Over the years, the growth of charter schools was joined by the growth of networks in order to augment the speed of systemic reform. The explosion of charter networks may have occurred in response to several trends in the educational environment.

First, individual charter schools have not had the rapid, large-scale impact originally intended by charter school reformers (Wohlstetter, Smith, & Farrell, 2013). Studies of student performance in charter schools have shown mixed results, and the intended innovations in educational instructional design, which is a stated goal of many state charter laws, is not occurring to the extent expected (Lubienski, 2003; Wohlstetter, Wenning, & Briggs, 1995). Most charter school principals possess a great deal of autonomy over the organization and its operations, thus making their decisions somewhat more consequential than those of their traditional counterparts (Bulkley, 2004; Gawlik, 2008; Wohlstetter & Chau, 2004).

While much has been written about the role of traditional public school principals in school succession (Datnow et al., 2002; Hargreaves, Moore, Fink, Brayman, & White, 2003), little is understood about the role of charter school principals, and how succession coupled with the process of socialization influences the success of charter schools. Thus, the current chapter explores the ways in which charter schools manage succession and control the socialization of individuals as they move into principalship roles. Using the theory of socialization developed by Van Maanen and Schein (1979), the study establishes a framework for investigating organizational socialization in charter schools.

CHALLENGES OF SCHOOL PRINCIPALSHIP

Given the increased demands for accountability as measured by student achievement, the job of the school principal has become more complex and more focused on instructional principalship (Crow, 2006; Pounder & Merrill, 2001). Accountability pressures as well as other factors (e.g., lack of support from the central office and low compensation) have contributed to decreasing interest in school principalship (Fuller & Young, 2009). Loeb, Kalogrides, & Horng (2010) found that applicants have become much more selective in where they are willing to work, as evidenced by school principals more often choosing to "work in easier-to-serve schools with favorable working conditions" (p. 205).

Principalship Challenges in Charter Schools

Several common characteristics of charter schools increase and complicate the responsibilities of principals. Data from a recent survey of charter school leaders show that principals often have difficulty fundraising, managing facilities, and negotiating with the traditional public school districts in which they are located, none of which are concerns for traditional public school principals (Campbell & Grubb, 2008). Although some charter school principals (typically those at schools in charter school networks, such as educational management organizations [EMOs] or nonprofit charter management organizations [CMOs]) receive strong principalship support from a central office and are relieved of tasks that do not relate directly to student learning (Goff, Mavrogordato, & Goldring, 2012), the principals of typical start-up charter schools cannot rely on a central office for support.

Stand-alone charter schools face many operational and financial challenges and have frequently closed because of financial and governance mismanagement issues (Center for Education Reform, 2014). Thus, in addition to the duties of traditional principals, the principals of stand-alone charter schools are responsible for finding and maintaining school facilities; handling finances; raising money; recruiting students; and negotiating relationships with boards, parents, and charter school authorizing agencies.

Charter school principals also face context-specific concerns ranging from economic, health, and cultural problems (Bush & Oduro, 2006) to expectations related to marketing and concerns related to accountability (Briggs, Bush, & Middlewood 2006; Walker & Qian, 2006).

Moreover, charter school principals must establish and maintain a school's vision, build trust between adults and children, manage resources, and balance pressures from both inside and outside the school (Campbell, Gross, & Lake, 2008). Finally, charter school principals may also experience role conflict as they address instructional, political, and public relations issues (Cowie & Crawford, 2008; Nelson, de la Colina, & Boone, 2008).

Thus far, researchers have concluded that the leadership differences between charter and traditional public schools stem from organizational features and inherent differences in governance (Goff et al., 2012). The existing literature does not address whether or not these differences in leadership practices could be explained by factors other than organizational features and governance. This chapter advances the literature in the field by highlighting a new set of differences between charter school leaders and their traditional counterparts—variation in the roles they assume.

Principalship Succession

Succession and socialization are complementary processes during which a new principal influences the existing culture of a school, and vice versa (Bengtson, Zepeda, & Parylo, 2013). Principalship succession is not a temporary concern, but rather a systematic issue in the public school system (Hargreaves & Fink, 2006). The need for schools to strategically plan and manage the succession of principals is well documented (Fink & Brayman, 2004, 2006; Hargreaves & Fink, 2006; Hargreaves et al., 2003; Hart, 1993). A comprehensive study of principalship succession (Hargreaves et al., 2003) found it to be one of the most significant variables affecting school climate and sustainability efforts in the school.

Documentation of the negative effects of principal transience has led to the creation of principalship induction and training programs in the hope that improved succession procedures will lead to lower levels of principal turnover. Although there is an extensive literature on succession (Hargreaves et al., 2003), there have been few attempts to analyze charter school succession planning *at the school level*. Given that nearly three-quarters of charter school principals express the desire to move on to new opportunities or retire within five years of service, school-level research on succession planning in charter schools is particularly important (Campbell et al., 2008).

Two central issues in principalship succession are whether a transition maintains continuity or provokes discontinuity, and the extent to which the succession is planned. The literature identifies distinct types of principalship succession. The first, *planned continuity*, occurs when the assignment of a new principal is guided by a detailed succession plan designed to sustain a predecessor's legacy. This type of succession plan is typically found in the most innovative schools, and when schools are implementing significant changes.

The second type of succession identified by researchers is *unplanned discontinuity and continuity*, in which there is a clear break with the achievements of a previous principal, but continuity in maintaining the status quo. This type of transition sometimes occurs when a principal from a more successful school is reassigned to a school facing a challenge (Hargreaves & Fink, 2006).

Socialization Framework

This study uses the six dimensions of the socialization process identified by Van Maanen and Schein (1979) to explore the strategies employed by charter schools and to produce a more nuanced understanding of how incoming charter school principals approach succession and are then socialized to adjust to the needs of the charter school. The first dimension, collective versus individual, refers to whether a group undergoes a common set of experiences and is subject to peer influences, or a single individual moves into a new role alone without the influence of colleagues in the field.

The second dimension examines the difference between formal and informal preparation. The former involves individuals receiving recognized training, such as professional preparation, while in the latter, socialization is embedded in the work. The third dimension distinguishes sequential socialization—a series of steps or stages that recruits are required to move through before assuming new responsibilities—from random socialization, which occurs when the path to a new principalship role is not well defined or formalized.

The fourth dimension contrasts fixed socialization, in which there is a timeline allowing upcoming principals to know when they will move into their new role, and variable socialization, in which there is no timeline. The fifth dimension, serial socialization versus disjunctive socialization, pertains to whether or not veteran principals of the organization groom new members for their roles.

Finally, investiture socialization occurs when organizations accept new members as they are, without changes, while divestiture socialization occurs when there is an attempt to change certain personal characteristics of the incoming individual.

Research Objectives

This chapter seeks to fill the gap in the literature on principalship succession and socialization in charter schools. Given the lack of previous research in this area and the methodological limitations of the current study, the research is exploratory and inductive in nature. This study used extensive data on three schools and their principals to fashion a rich, thick description of the ways in which the focal charter schools manage principalship succession and socialization.

I focus on examining four issues in particular:

1. The schools' succession plans
2. The extent to which managing principalship succession is a priority for the charter school principals in the sample
3. How the sampled charter school principals experience socialization within their schools
4. The relationship between the role of the principal, and the practices and processes that lead to socialization

Overview of Charter Schools in Florida

Charter schools have emerged as a popular option in the school choice movement and Florida is a leader among the states that use charter schools as a reform measure (Center for Educational Reform, 2014). Close to 653 public charter schools in Florida serve more than 150,000 students (Center for Education Reform, 2014). The majority of Florida's charter schools are free-standing (managed by individual members or organizations within the community).

Nationally, 10.6 percent (639) of all charter schools are conversion charter schools, while the majority (89.4 percent [5,364]) are start-up charter schools. In Florida, only 3.1 percent (18) of all charter schools are conversion charters, while 96.9 percent (558) are start-up charter schools (National Alliance for Public Charter Schools, 2013).

The Florida legislature, in authorizing the creation of public charter schools, established the following guiding principles: high standards of student achievement combined with increased parental choice; the alignment of responsibility with accountability; and ensuring parents receive information on their children's reading levels and educational progress. Charter schools are intended to improve student learning; increase learning opportunities, especially for low-performing students and with regard to reading; and measure learning outcomes.

Charter schools may also create innovative measurement tools, provide competition to stimulate improvement in traditional schools, expand the capacity of the public school system, and mitigate the educational impact created by the development of new residential units (Florida Department of Education, 2015).

METHODS

Study Design

Case studies can be an effective tool for understanding the research question at hand. The duration and depth of the study provides important initial and exploratory information about the process of principalship succession and socialization in charter schools. Data collection occurred in three elementary charter schools in Florida over the course of the 2012–2013 academic year. Data sources included semi-structured interviews and follow-up interviews with current and former charter school principals, field notes, and school improvement plans.

Case Selection

Purposeful sampling was employed to select a group of charter schools that varied in geographical location, school context, student demographics, and school performance. The schools selected met these criteria:

- An elementary school (because principalship succession appears to be concentrated at this organizational level)
- A student population of 250 or more
- A start-up charter school in existence for at least five years
- Received school grades for the 2011–2012 year
- Employed a principal who either recently left or was planning on leaving

The original sample included four charter schools in Florida—two in a northern county and two in a southern county. Midway through the study, however, one of the southern schools withdrew. The final sample included three schools, which I call Purple, Red, and White charter schools. Three current and two former principals from these charter schools were interviewed, and two of the current principals also participated in follow-up interviews.

Charter school board presidents were twice invited to participate in interviews with the researcher, but all declined. Thus, the study focuses on the perspective of the principals. In order to understand the six dimensions of socialization outlined by Van Maanen & Schein (1979), the interview questions posed to the principals focused on how incoming charter school principals approach succession and how they were socialized to adjust to the needs of the charter school. The study sample included principals that were certified, had been employed as a principal (in the focus school or another school) for at least one year, and had recently left or had plans to leave.

Data Collection and Analysis

The interviews with charter school principals, which were conducted at the chosen schools, were standardized following a semi-structured interview protocol. Both the wording and the sequence of questions were predetermined. This procedure reduced interviewer bias; however, because standardized questions tend to constrain the responses of interviewees, probes were often used when appropriate to encourage the respondents to expound on their initial responses.

The use of standardized, semi-structured interview questions allowed the comparison of responses across interviewees (Patton, 1990). At the completion of the interview, the interviewer summarized the data and allowed respondents to immediately correct errors of fact or to challenge interpretations (Erlandson, Harris, Skipper, & Allen, 1993). This credibility or member check was used to assess the trustworthiness of the data collection. All interviews were tape-recorded, transcribed, stored, and analyzed using NVivo 9.0. Interviews lasted from 60 to 90 minutes.

In addition to conducting interviews, I observed and documented staff meetings, professional development sessions, classes, and informal interactions between charter principals and their staff. I recorded both descriptive and reflective field notes on interviews and observations over a span of several months. Thorough narratives were created for each person involved in a social situation and brief updates were added in later field notes as people and details about them changed. School improvement plans were also reviewed and coded to determine whether succession plans were included or addressed.

The constant comparative analysis method was employed because it is compatible with the inductive, concept-building orientation of qualitative research. In this method, the researcher compares one data point (e.g., one interview) to all other data points (Glaser, 1965). The constant comparative method involves separating the data into discrete "incidents" (Glaser & Strauss, 1967) or "units" (Lincoln & Guba, 1985) and using descriptive and explanatory categories to code each of these units.

The descriptive and explanatory categories undergo changes in both definition and content as the researcher's understanding of the properties of the categories and the relationships between categories develops and becomes more refined over the course of the analytical process. As the categories were refined and subcategories were created, patterns among the categories emerged. I also relied on peer debriefing to enhance the accuracy of the account by asking experts in the field to review and ask questions about the protocols and the qualitative study.

RESULTS

The findings are divided into three themes: the importance of succession planning, teacher leadership development, and principalship styles and culture. The findings focus on the schools' succession plans, the extent to which managing principalship succession is a priority for the charter school principals in the sample, how the sampled charter school principals experience socialization within their schools, and the relationship between the role of principal and the practices and processes that lead to socialization.

Overview of Focal Charter Schools

Three charter schools (Purple, Red, and White) were included in the final study. Table 5.1 presents basic statistical information about each school collected in 2012–2013.

Purple Charter School and Red Charter School are located in a medium-sized county in northern Florida. The population of the northern county is approximately 300,000 and is moderately diverse: 30 percent of residents are African American, 6 percent are Latino/a, and 5 percent are Asian American

Table 5.1. Demographic Profiles of the Focal Charter Schools

	North		South
	Purple	Red	White
Number of Students	271	663	375
% White	69.5	53.1	44.5
% African American	22.1	33.8	20.0
% Latino/a	7.7	4.5	25.6
% Asian American	5.5	1.7	3.2
% Disabled	15.9	9.8	16.5
% Free or Reduced-price Lunch	15.1	30.3	39.2
% English Language Learners	2.2	2.3	1.1
School's Performance Rating (A = highest performance, F = failing)	A	C	B

(U.S. Census Bureau, 2012). Approximately 20 percent of the population lives below the poverty line (U.S. Census Bureau, 2012) and, although the majority of residents designated English as their primary language, a minority of the residents spoke Spanish and French Creole as their primary language.

White Charter School is located in a larger southern county with a population of approximately 1.6 million; 20 percent of residents are African American, 16 percent are Latino/a, and 2 percent are Asian American (U.S. Census Bureau, 2012). The primary languages spoken by residents of this county include Spanish and French Creole, and 11 percent of the population lives below the poverty line (U.S. Census Bureau, 2012).

The sampled charter schools serve from 271 to 663 elementary students. The percentage of students who are economically disadvantaged varies significantly, from 15.1 percent at Purple School to almost 40 percent at White School. Whites were the largest group at each of the three schools. At Purple and Red schools, African Americans were the largest minority group, while at White School, Latino/as were the largest minority group.

All public schools in Florida are graded annually based on student performance, state assessments, and the percentage of students making learning gains; each charter school is assigned a letter grade (A through F, where A represents the highest performance rating and F represents failing). Among the focal schools, Purple School received the highest rating (A), while White School received a B, and Red School received a C.

Overview of the Focal Principals

Three current principals were invited to participate in this study. The first, Principal White, was one of the original founders of the White Charter School, a small urban charter school that has been in existence for 11 years. Principal White was a Caucasian woman in her 50s who taught elementary school in the West Palm Beach District prior to founding the school. When the White Charter School's original acting leader, who had served for approximately one year, stepped down for medical reasons, Principal White volunteered to act as interim director. During her initial nine-month term, the board conducted a search but did not find a candidate whose required salary they could afford, so they asked White if she would consider serving as the school's leader on a permanent basis. While serving as the school's leader, she obtained a master's degree in administrative leadership.

Principal White's main concern at the inception of her appointment was academic achievement, specifically, how the school could increase and then sustain its academic performance. After a 10-year tenure, she announced that she would be leaving White Charter School to retire.

The principal of Purple Charter School had a background similar to that of the principal of White Charter School. Principal Purple was also a Caucasian woman in her 50s. She, too, started as one of the founders of her charter school. The previous principal had retired five years earlier, and the assistant principal had served as interim principal until Principal Purple took over the reins.

Principal Purple had served as an elementary teacher at Purple Charter School for seven years before becoming interested in administration. She eventually became a teacher leader for the school, assumed more administrative responsibilities, and received her credentials in administration. When the position of principal became available, the school conducted a national search; Principal Purple was one of several applicants, and was eventually hired by the charter school board. Her primary focus was maintaining the charter school's mission and purpose.

Purple Charter School had enjoyed success as an A graded school, and Principal Purple wanted to maintain its status. She had plans to retire in the next several years but wondered how Purple Charter School would continue to maintain its high performance level without a succession plan in place. She felt strongly that someone would rise through the ranks of teacher leadership in the school and eventually follow in her footsteps.

The last principal, Principal Red, was a member of the charter management organization (CMO) in Florida. Principal Red was an African American woman in her 40s. She had recently transferred to Red Charter School and had served as principal for a year and a half at the time of the interview. She had undergone principals' roundtable training, which was offered by the CMO and led to certification recognition through the CMO. Prior to her training, she served as a middle school teacher for five years at a traditional public school. She then assumed a teaching position with the CMO and taught for an additional three years before entering the administrative training program offered by the CMO.

Principal Red served as an assistant principal for two years at another charter school before accepting a transfer to Red Charter School. Upon her transfer, she assumed the role of principal of Red Charter School and was charged with the difficult task of turning the school around. The charter school suffered from low student performance, and Principal Red was specifically brought in to remedy that. Because she was relatively new to the position, she was able to offer insights into the socialization process she had undergone as a new charter school administrator.

Importance of Succession Planning

The comments of two of the three current charter school principals addressed aspects of fixed versus variable socialization. In general, the charter school principals expressed little to no concern about succession planning and management, suggesting that there was a high degree of variable socialization when a new principal was hired. Because neither the phenomenon of succession nor the need for a new principal was necessarily predictable, the time frame for entering the principalship role was ambiguous, and thus fixed socialization was far less common among the charter schools in this study. Most of the charters did not have a pressing need to have a fixed timeline for succession.

One reason principals placed little emphasis on succession planning and used variable rather than fixed socialization was that these schools had experienced somewhat low levels of principalship turnover, and the principals had assumed their positions somewhat recently. Purple School had no timeline in place to forecast when the next principal would succeed the current one. When asked if the staff had engaged in discussions about succession plans, the principal replied: "No. Because I think there are still board members who don't want it to be an assumed succession . . . they don't want that next person to automatically be it. They want to know as an entity that they've got the best person who was interested in being here in this position." Thus, the principal of Purple School asserted that board members might assume that having a succession plan would mean having a predetermined prospective principal. The board wanted to conduct discussions before inviting candidates to interview for the position. When the current principal was hired, the board had conducted a national search.

Both of the former charter school principals interviewed commented on the importance of schools identifying a new principal who was the "right fit" and possessed the appropriate attitudes, values, and mannerisms to fill the role. These comments reflect the formal socialization and qualifications (teacher certification and administrative experience) that school principals often sought in incoming principals. Thus, formal succession planning might be too confining for charter schools, which may be seeking to maximize flexibility.

Formal socialization did occur in at least one of the focal charter schools. Some of the principals who had received their formal training and certification within a charter network had to wait for a principalship position to open. This was true of Red Charter School, which relied on formal training provided by the network. When asked about the biggest obstacles to succession planning, the Red Charter School principal explained:

> Well, I would say that probably the biggest obstacle for our school would still be that it is not top-down. So, even if there is someone in the school, which we try to promote from within, we have to realize what [that] means within this school. So even though I may think Stacey next door will be an excellent AP [assistant principal], that's opened up to all of the school. And the way our

hiring structure works is that we have done it by task force. So, there is a task force with different individuals that sit and actually select the principal, and then the candidate is presented to the board for their approval or denial.

This process prevented Red Charter School from selecting one individual to be groomed for the position. Principals who had been developed from within the school often had to compete with both internal and external candidates. For example, Red Charter School used a process that combined both formal and informal socialization. Although they searched outside the charter network when hiring a new principal, they also attempted to promote individual teachers from within the organization. Red School initiated a principal roundtable, at which aspiring principals gathered to discuss matters relevant to leading a school (e.g., budgets and instructional principalship).

Observations and field notes indicated that the roundtable provided an opportunity for aspiring principals to problem solve as a team and to address challenges that they might face in the future. Often, a problem or issue was presented to the candidates, and they would have to strategize about the best possible solutions and identify stakeholders that needed to be involved. The chance to develop the confidence and knowledge necessary to provide critical feedback was important for these individuals who sought to take on principalship roles in charter schools.

Red School's roundtable eventually grew into a Principal Candidate School, at which aspiring principals engaged in a sequence of activities that prepared them to assume a principalship role at a charter school. As the Red School principal noted, if the charter network did not have enough principalship positions for all those who attended the Principal Candidate School, well-prepared individuals would have to leave the network to continue their principalship development.

In some respects, then, implementing a succession plan that promotes the development and selection of new principals may be counterproductive if the number of principals being prepared exceeds the projected number of principalship openings.

Teacher Leadership Development

The complex and demanding task of being a charter school principal have led schools to develop internal support structures for leadership development. Although university programs serve as one form of formal sequential socialization for educators seeking principalship positions, a training gap remains; the need for internal leadership development has become apparent as charter schools seek candidates with the leadership abilities and skills needed to succeed in the context of a particular charter school and community. The charter school principals in this study recognized some level of need for the development of principals, and identified aspects of teacher leadership development as their formal and informal sequential tactics for socialization and succession.

Several models have emerged for developing teacher leaders (Wynne, 2001). Generally, these models are grouped into two broad pathways: role-based approaches and community-based approaches. The current data confirm that teachers began to define teacher leadership in terms of traditional roles with which they were familiar, such as union representatives, department heads, and committee chairs.

Hence, initial efforts in this area focused on assigning teachers to formal leadership roles within schools (Odell, 1997); this process included assigning roles such as lead, mentor, and master teachers, and adopting forms of differentiated teacher staffing that defined a variety of specific career paths.

Purple Charter School adopted a role-based approach to leadership development; the principal commented that the school was "growing them from within." While the principal noted that a change in principalship "was not in anyone's forethought right now," she explained that she sought to identify individual teachers who indicated that they would like to move into principalship positions or showed principalship potential. The principal of Purple Charter School spoke extensively about the leadership roles in the school (e.g., board chair, assistant principal, chair of the school advisory council) and the efforts to fill those positions with teachers. The focus of these leadership positions was anchored in the day-to-day activities of the charter school. For example, teachers' leadership roles included mentor, peer coach, lead teacher, curriculum developer, and administrative intern.

The former principal of the Purple School had served from 1998 to 2011, and the current principal commented, "I didn't feel like she could [move on] because [she] didn't feel like she had the principalship in place she wanted to leave the school to." Having a principal that understood the mission and purpose of the organization and could carry its vision forward was pivotal for the succession process for this charter school.

The vision of the school was intimately tied to the success it had enjoyed over the past several years and to having a leader who would carry on that tradition was critical to its ongoing success. The current principal of the Purple Charter School commented that her "job was to just keep it on because we were highly successful before I came on board." Her perception was that "nothing needed to be changed to enhance the school because it was already successful."

The White Charter School used strategies similar to those employed by the Purple Charter School—both schools groomed current teachers for future principalship positions. The White School principal explained:

> Well, right now I'm taking one of my teachers who has been here for nine years and she actually wants to go into the principalship track and she's doing that right now. Last year, she started on issues so she's a teacher on assignment. She is getting principalship-like, administrative-type duties to do, and [we are] training her into those positions so every year she's learning a little bit more.

At Red School and Purple School, the work of developing principals occurred largely through informal mechanisms, which signals a departure from more traditional forms of leadership development. In the past decade, several new approaches to teacher leadership have surfaced (Smylie, Conley, & Marks, 2002). The community-based approach regards the leadership *acts* rather than the leadership *role* as the defining essence of teacher leadership. Community-based teacher leadership acknowledges the realities of practice for teacher leaders as much more challenging and complex.

This strategy shifts attention away from individual and role-based conceptions of leadership; rather than focusing on the formal empowerment of individual teachers, the strategy emphasizes leadership tasks, behaviors, and functions, as well as the importance of the teaching context and the organizational development of the school (Odell, 1997). Thus, teacher leadership is not experienced in isolation, but rather is linked with development in schools (Zimpher, 1988). Teacher leadership is formulated less as a role and more as a mind-set, a way of being, acting, and thinking as a learner within a community of learners.

White Charter School displayed community-based teacher leadership. For example, the principal of White Charter School discussed creating an inclusive environment for teachers; she explained, "I take into consideration all the information I've gotten from everybody. And I try to give the teachers a share in that decision-making because I want them to feel like this is their school, they're stakeholders here." Observations of interactions between the principals and teachers confirmed this shared decision-making between teachers and the principal.

For the principal of White Charter School, the goal of creating an inclusive decision-making environment was coupled with a contextual understanding of the organizational climate. She emphasized that Sharon, the teacher leader, "knows what built this school and made it a success; she's seen how I've operated it for it to be successful; she knows the history and background because she's been here for a long time." Therefore, installing a principal with institutional knowledge of the school influenced the socialization process by ensuring adherence to the inclusive decision-making process and supporting the replication of the current principalship style.

Unlike Purple School and White School, Red Charter School defined leadership development more formally and as consisting of preparation processes supported by the charter school network. Lead teachers, assistant principals, and other central office principals were trained as a group. The training occurred outside employees' daily jobs, and the Principal Candidate School was used to develop a pool of candidates. The purpose of the program was to cultivate leadership skills and increase opportunities for young professionals within the network. Because these individuals were separated from other staff, Red School's socialization process was formal rather than informal. As the principal of Red School explained:

> I held several leadership roles within [the school]. I served on different task forces. And then we have a process for principals to grow within the school, which in prior years was called "principals' roundtable." So, I attended every roundtable that we had, and that is where a bunch of our principals come together. It really grows our principals and kind of molds them into being principals. So, it's a session where we get together, we go over human resources, the budget and different things that principals would come across in the actual role. So, I attended every principals' roundtable that we had and then, over the year, the principal roundtable turned into Principal Candidate School and I attended Principal Candidate School as well.

This process reflects the value that Red School placed on leadership development, and signals a departure from the informal teacher leadership development framework utilized by the other two charter schools. The use of specific activities to improve the knowledge, skills, and abilities of participants helped clarify the goals of leadership development for aspiring principals at Red School.

The collective socialization process consisted of a common set of experiences during which participants were influenced by their peers; in addition, the process provided a unique opportunity for aspiring principals to problem solve as a team. The process reinforced the importance of having teacher principals in the school, and created a culture of inquiry about teachers' knowledge and practice within the school.

Principalship Styles and Culture

Each particular combination of these socialization factors entails a specific set of pressures, cultural expectations, social issues, and values that contribute to how the principalship role develops in a school. All three charter schools displayed characteristics of collective socialization (socialization in which individuals share a common set of experiences and are influenced by their peers). This collective socialization, however, manifested itself differently in each of the three schools, varying by principalship style and the cultural context of the school. For example, the principal of White Charter School described herself as a "collaborative principal."

While she acknowledged that she ultimately made the decisions affecting the school, she noted that she always incorporated information provided by the teachers. She explained:

> I try to give the teachers and the staff a share in the decision-making because I want them to feel like this is their school; they're stakeholders here too. And I can't do that by myself; this has to be done by the teachers and staff. So I can't operate under a dictatorship, and I wouldn't want somebody else to work under that condition. I'm not a micro-manager at all.

My observations of White School principal's formal and informal interactions with teachers confirmed her self-assessment. Teachers at White School provided input when decisions were made, and provided firsthand knowledge of the charter school's day-to-day operations. The principal of White Charter School asserted that outside successors do not have the information needed to manage their day-to-day activities and relate to teachers in a way that elicits cooperation. This principal was familiar with efforts to introduce an "outsider" to the school. She explained:

> I did try last year to bring a teacher from outside the district that was already in the assistant principal pool, and it didn't work out. The teacher that came in from the outside had her own agenda. She wanted to go into administration. She was going to come in as the AP, and when I retired, she was going to take my job. She was going to move the school into another building, and she had her own agenda of what she wanted to do. She didn't come in and let herself become accepted and find out what the school was about first.

In this instance, the school initially used divestiture socialization to eliminate certain characteristics of the "outsider" and reconcile the behaviors of the district teacher to the demands and culture of the charter school.

Although the White School principal reported receiving applications from several candidates within the district, she asserted that the "district mind-set" of these candidates would make it difficult for them to transition to the charter school culture and adopt a collaborative approach toward principalship. She talked at length about how the current principal in training was very familiar with the history of the charter school, the factors that made the school successful, and the school's particular culture. Thus, the data show that, when developing a principal from within, White School employed investiture socialization (accepting the current teacher principal as is, without demanding she make changes to her principalship style).

In addition, there was a direct flow of communication between the current principal and the teacher principal, and this open communication allowed for intimate knowledge of the charter school operation through administrative duties. The expectation was that the teacher leader would "assume principalship of the charter school when I [the current principal] retired or resigned."

The principal of the Purple Charter School described the school's culture as a "very strong community, [a] familial, respectful culture. We honor each other's differences and our students are given [a] voice." As described above, Purple School is a grass-roots charter school started by parents and educators whose goal was to create a school with a strong emphasis on culture and learning. The Purple School principal noted that the lack of principalship turnover was an extremely important component of the school's success.

She explained that "because [the school] was the result of a grown grass-roots movement, we don't have a company behind us saying to do this model and it'll work. Instead, we had a whole bunch of dreamers who said, 'We think we can do education in a different way.'"

This mission prompted the principal to hire staff members who would adopt the school's culture and believe in the school's mission. When asked to characterize her principalship style, the principal of Purple Charter School responded, "Inclusive." She continued, "I want input from lots of people; [however] I will make the hard decisions when I have to, even if it's against the input because I have to look at the whole rather than whatever individual is coming to me."

The principal of Purple School spoke passionately about having served as a classroom teacher prior to becoming a principal, and reported that her knowledge of the classroom informed her current work as a principal. She continued, discussing "the shift [in the focus of] principalship" that many charter school principals have confronted in the last two years. As mentioned by the Red Charter principal, in the past charter school principals were more focused on the managerial aspect of running a school, but recently the emphasis has shifted to instructional aspects. This shift was due, in part, to a broader focus on accountability and the implementation of Common Core standards.

The principal of Red Charter School spoke fervently about the role of principalship and its relationship to socialization. The Red School is part of an established network that embraces a student-centered philosophy based on six measures of success: parent choice; economic sustainability; positive character development; academic achievement; school development; and shared values of justice, integrity, and fun. A core task for the principal of Red School was ensuring that teachers had confidence in her ability to lead while allowing them to maintain their professional autonomy. She described herself as an "instructional principal" who helped "grow" teachers via professional development and modeling. She described some of the ways in which she led the teachers: "So even when I'm in classrooms I like to provide examples of what it is I'm looking for, so I spend a lot of time doing and exhibiting the behavior I want the staff to see. Our focus [is] the students, and now we need to live the school philosophy and make sure that the reasons people choose our school is because we're doing the things that hold true."

The Red Charter School, unlike the other two focal schools, was under some pressure to improve student performance and increase the school grade assigned by the state of Florida. The principal felt an urgent need to implement effective instructional strategies that would lead to a better assessment and improved scores on school performance criteria.

The principal of Red School described holding a series of principalship roles as part of the Principal Candidate School, and noted that she had been recognized as a national teacher of the year. Upon assuming the role of school principal, her initial goal was to make teachers familiar and comfortable with her. After about six months, she began to set instructional and achievement expectations for the teachers. She commented:

> So, they knew what my expectations were. They knew certain things were there that they weren't used to, like always being in the classroom. They understood that I will be in the classroom but I didn't impress that upon them at the time. My vision of where I wanted the school to go right then and there was present, but I wanted them to be comfortable when they saw me in the classroom and to continue with their teaching methods.

Based on my observations, the principal of Red School was present in classrooms about five hours every day, and she modeled specific instructional methods to help teachers with the challenges they faced in their classrooms. She also arranged for teachers to meet in teams to outline goals and visions for their students in terms of data-driven instruction; my observations indicated that the teachers supported the new principal's instructional approach. They were receptive in team meetings and asked questions and were engaged in discussion. There was also a tremendous amount of interaction between the principal and the teachers, which reinforced their exchanges, and this reinforcement was critical for successful socialization.

DISCUSSION

This exploratory case study had two primary goals: (1) to examine the practices surrounding principalship succession—how principals are chosen, whether schools have implemented succession plans, and the priority placed on managing principalship succession—in a sample of charter schools in Florida; and (2) to analyze how principals experience socialization and how succession planning practices affect principalship socialization in these schools.

The results reveal variation among the schools with respect to preparation for principalship transitions and subsequent socialization. At Purple Charter

School, the new principal was charged with sustaining and nurturing the school's current performance and direction. Her approach as an inclusive principal included accepting the status quo in order to maintain the existing knowledge, strategies, and mission of the school. In contrast, the principal of Red Charter School was charged with changing the direction of the school. She employed a role innovation response, in which she sought to change the teachers' instructional strategies and place more emphasis on data-driven instruction and content-rich curricula. In preparation for an upcoming transfer of principalship, the principal of White Charter School was grooming a teacher principal to assume the role of principal and to incorporate and sustain the existing culture of the charter school. All three school principals stressed that developing aspiring principals was an important aspect of the succession and socialization process. Approaches to principalship development ranged from a more formal approach in Red School to a more informal approach in White and Purple Charter Schools.

This study advances the scholarly understanding of how charter schools prepare for succession and principalship socialization through teacher leadership. Teacher leadership in White Charter School was characterized by community-based strategies, including a broadening of socialization activities ingrained in the school's culture and vision. The teacher leaders at this site engaged in targeted work but were more removed, completing administrative tasks and focusing on a broad segment of tasks affiliated with the charter school community. Although there has been a shift away from role-based initiatives (Smylie et al., 2002), the current results reveal they are still present at White Charter School.

At the Purple Charter School, teacher principalship was guided by a set of role-based strategies, which were deeply embedded in a framework of leadership that depends on individual empowerment. These two pathways to teacher principalship suggest there may be different potential outcomes of "growing" teachers from within a school. Moreover, the role-based teacher principals at Purple Charter School were accountable (or responsive) to their respective administrators, while the community-based teacher principals at the White Charter School were accountable (or responsive) to their colleagues.

Having an organizational socialization plan that is sequential and incorporates divestiture processes may strengthen the experiences of new principals (Hart, 1993; Weindling, 2000) and encourage successful socialization. The Principal Candidate School at Red Charter School defined a distinct process for training aspiring principals, which allowed participants to become acquainted with their new role as a principal and develop the skills and awareness needed to be a successful principal.

In addition, the cultures of Purple School and White School created a situation in which "group-think" might occur. Although both schools were currently performing well, attention must be given when a comfort level has been reached about divesting a former principal for a new one (Browne-Ferrigno, 2003; Normore, 2004), because this development may lead to new forms of socialization.

Finally, the issue of principalship succession and its relationship to school performance must be mentioned. Previous research (Robinson, Lloyd, & Rowe, 2008; Wahlstrom, Seashore, Leithwood, & Anderson, 2010) has found that the principalship has an impact on school performance; in addition, earlier studies have indicated that unplanned principal succession has a negative effect on school performance (Fink & Brayman, 2004). These findings lead to three potential outcomes.

The first is that principalship succession will positively influence school performance. If a new principal can control organizational outcomes, attributions of principal causation of organizational events support the notion that principalship change will have a positive effect on performance (Miskel & Cosgrove, 1985). The second possibility is that succession will create instability, and thus decrease organizational effectiveness. The third possibility is that succession will play no causal role in organizational effectiveness.

Although the current study does not explicitly address the relationship between succession and school performance, the results do hint that succession does not necessarily lead to a decrease in organizational effectiveness. Both Purple School and Red School had relatively new principals in place, and neither had experienced a decline in their school grade after the principalship transition.

IMPLICATIONS FOR PRACTICE

The results provide deep, rich descriptions of the processes of succession and socialization at the focal schools. These results are exploratory, and provide a conceptual/analytic framework that can be used to guide future practices on other charter schools and networks. This study can serve as a foundation for future practice, which should (1) highlight the practices associated with using teacher leadership as a stepping stone to building-level principalship, and (2) compare network-based and stand-alone charter schools with respect to principalship development.

Specifically, the study of teacher leadership can serve to inform which role-based and community-based practices facilitate the building of a foundation for future leaders of charter schools. Current charter school leaders must encourage current teachers interested in administration to nurture those skills. As demonstrated by the Principal Candidate School, CMOs are in a unique position to tailor future teachers for the role of principal. As networks prepare future leaders, they must collaborate with research-based universities to credential network programs and certify these programs with the state.

While the current findings indicate that charter schools differ in the degree to which they plan and manage principal succession, more investigation is needed to determine how these succession processes and their effects vary by school type (e.g., public/private, suburban/rural).

This study suggests that, although principalship succession is an important issue, some charter schools do not have a consistent plan in place to ensure that succession does not adversely affect student performance. Ideally, a careful plan for principalship succession should be incorporated into the school improvement plan. Such plans provide considerable lead time, develop shared understanding and commitment among faculty, and synchronize the new principal's knowledge with the knowledge of the departing principal, thus allowing the new leader to build on the previous achievements of the school. However, the majority of the data gathered thus far indicate that most succession events at charter schools are unplanned and somewhat arbitrary.

Unplanned succession often impedes efforts toward school improvement. The chances of a successful succession are increased when all participants, rather than only one or two individuals, have a vested interest in a school's success. Ideal succession plans address the composition and development of the principalship team in a charter school to ensure that responsibility will be shared (Hargreaves et al., 2003). Incorporating succession plans into school improvement plans would produce beneficial documentation and serve as an important step toward the successful implementation of a new principal.

NOTE

1. Some charter schools are part of networks known as charter management organizations (CMOs). A CMO is a nonprofit organization that manages multiple charter schools with a common mission and instructional design, and has a home management team that offers ongoing support to its schools.

Conclusion

New Looks at Charter Principal Leadership

Dana L. Bickmore and Marytza A. Gawlik

How charter school principals engage in the work of leadership is the focus of this book, the second in a two-part series. Research articles selected for this second volume reinforced themes presented in the first, such as charter principal autonomy and the additional tasks faced by charter principals (Bickmore & Gawlik, 2017). More importantly, this second book examined specific policy issues encountered by charter school principals not previously detailed in the research.

As in the first book, the researchers used qualitative research methods to provide storied examinations across multiple contexts to highlight the work of charter principals. This concluding chapter summarizes how authors have expanded the literature related to charter school principals and addresses themes that emerged across the chapters.

TEASING OUT SPECIFIC CHARTER PRINCIPAL LEADERSHIP ISSUES

Principal leadership is a complicated set of knowledge, skills, and dispositions rallied to address varied and multifaceted issues faced by principals (Hull, 2012). Researchers have explored a number of issues that traditional principals encounter, generating a growing body of evidence to guide effective practice (Leithwood, Seashore-Louis, Anderson, & Wahlstrom, 2004). Few studies, however, have explicitly examined how charter principals face and meet specific issues that may be similar or different from those of traditional principals.

Authors in this book move the understanding of charter principal leadership forward by highlighting and describing three specific issues charter principals confront. These issues outline how charter principals (1) deal with accountability demands, (2) engage in teacher evaluation and development, and (3) are selected and socialized into their jobs as charter leaders. Although these issues are not unique to charter principals, describing the context and practices of these charter principals as they maneuvered through these three issues provides a clearer picture of charter principal leadership.

Accountability Demands

Mavrogordato, Goldring, and Smrekar in chapter 1 described the various tensions experienced by four charter principals as they balanced the autonomy afforded them with various accountability issues. Accountability was not defined strictly as state-mandated accountability testing. Instead, the authors described accountability in terms of charter organizational expectations and needs, as well as policy accountability demands. Principals were accountable for enacting the school mission, aligning curriculum and instruction to the mission, balancing decisions to charter board preferences, budgeting limited resources, hiring and compensating staff, and meeting state accountability requirements.

Although each principal expressed that they had a great deal of autonomy, more than that afforded traditional school principals, tensions arose between the autonomy these principals could exercise and the accountability they encountered. Mavrogordato and colleagues described variations in how these leaders used their autonomy to deal with these constraints. By describing how principals varied in their use of autonomy in relationship to the demands of organizational accountability, Mavrogordato and colleagues provide a more expansive understanding of charter principal autonomy than does much of the literature surrounding charter schools.

Teacher Evaluation and Development

In three chapters, authors explored how charter principals engaged in teacher evaluation and development (Miranda & Felber-Smith, chapter 2; Reid, chapter 3; Coghlan & Mintrop, chapter 4). To date, little has been written about how charter principals evaluate or develop their teachers. In these three studies, principals implemented state-mandated evaluation systems or grants with structured, designed systems to evaluate and/or develop teachers.

In each study, tensions arose between the systems implemented and the underlying intent of the policy or grant. The overarching theme from these three chapters suggests charter principals used the autonomy and flexibility afforded them to adapt teacher evaluation and development systems based on local goals, culture, and their leadership styles.

Reid suggested that perhaps the principals needed further training on how to implement the system such that policy intentions would be realized. Alternately, Coghlan and Mintrop sided with principal decisions to adapt and reject parts of the performance systems to protect the culture and the core mission of the school. The ability to adapt and innovate is a mainstay of the charter movement, and these chapters highlight the variations in implementing policies related to teacher evaluation, development, and compensation when principals have the power to make decisions at the school level.

Succession Planning

Gawlik (chapter 5) investigated charter principal succession. The topic of principal change and succession has growing importance as the charter movement progresses into its third decade and a greater number of founding principals leave their schools. Two issues related to charter principal succession surfaced from this research. First, even though principals touted the importance of succession planning, there was limited specific planning for principal change. Second, these charter principals were socialized into their roles through a collective socialization process from within the charter school or chartering organization.

These two findings are similar to those found in traditional schools (Hargreaves, Moore, Fink, Brayman, & White, 2003); little formal succession planning exists, and principals are generally socialized within the school rather than through formal training processes. Gawlik suggests that for charter schools, this informal process might be an advantage as "formal succession planning might be too confining for charter schools, which may be seeking to maximize flexibility." Flexibility allows boards to change the direction of the school through principal change.

However, Gawlik also suggests that employing collective socialization may lead to "group-think," which can stifle innovation. One of the major tenets of charter schooling is innovation. If future charter principals are only exposed to the ideas and values within a stand-alone or charter organization, there may be more conformity than innovation.

THEMES EMERGING ACROSS CHAPTERS

While the research outlined in these chapters exposed specific leadership issues faced by charter principals, several themes emerged across the studies. These themes include charter principal autonomy, how principals implement policy, principal preparation and development, and variations in principal leadership based on the type of charter organization.

Principal Autonomy

Since inception, one of the foundational elements of charter schooling has been the autonomy given teachers and administrator to manage and lead schools (Campbell & Gross, 2008). The research described in each chapter suggests that autonomy permeates how charter principals engaged in their work. The autonomy afforded these principals was a fundamental ingredient as they maneuvered through and around the issues they encountered.

Although Mavrogordato, Goldring, and Smrekar in chapter 1 pointed to organizational constraints that may limit charter principal's autonomy, findings from all other chapters validate that charter principals have the autonomy and flexibility to change, adjust, and adapt processes, structures, and policies when confronting leadership issues.

Miranda and Felber-Smith (chapter 2) and Coghlan and Mintrop (chapter 4) described how individual charter principals used their autonomy to adjust and adapt how they implemented structured grant programs that provided additional funding for teachers, teacher leader's roles, and professional development. Implementation by principals varied based on their personal background, philosophies, school culture, and perceived needs of their schools.

Reid (chapter 3) portrayed how principal autonomy, in combination with school context and each principal's personal priorities, resulted in wide variations in how state-mandated evaluations systems were implemented. Gawlik (chapter 5) even outlines how principals use their autonomy to socialize future administrators. Authors for each chapter confirmed that charter principals have greater autonomy than do their traditional school counterparts.

Policy Implementation

In four chapters, authors specifically discussed how principals use their autonomy to interpret, mediate, and adapt state and federal policy (chapters 1, 2, 3, and 4). This capacity to adapt policy may create tensions and issues for principals. The autonomy afforded charter principals is, as Reid suggests, a "double-edged sword." On the one hand, charter principals in these studies were able to mediate and adapt state and federal policies for what they perceived to be for the betterment of the school. This puts a great deal of pressure and weight on the decisions of charter principals, particularly of stand-alone charter schools, as they maneuver through the political and legal implications of policy adaption.

The other edge of the sword is the public's intent related to policy. How far can or should charter principals stray from the intent of public policies? Although researchers have explored the tension between policy intent and implementation in schools (Elmore, 2004), the autonomy allowed charter principals extends this discussion.

State charter policies provide charter schools, and by extension principals, autonomy and flexibility with the goal of promoting innovation (Wohlstetter, Smith, & Farrell, 2013). At the same time, polices are also put in place as levers to improve practice, as well as to protect the safety and rights of students and employees. These competing intents put the principal squarely in the middle of this rather precarious process.

Charter Principal Preparation and Development

Beyond the tension faced by charter principals as they mediate and implement policy, collectively the authors of these chapters have provided evidence that the charter principal may face different issues than traditional principals, or face similar issues with greater complexity. Although traditional principals also deal with the topics outlined by the researchers in this book—accountability demands, teacher evaluation and development, and succession planning—charter principals in the studies reported in this text, for the most part, did not have the support and guidance often garnered from district staffs.

This lack of support confirms previous research related to charter principals receiving less support yet higher demands than would be experienced by traditional principals (Cannata, Thombre, & Thomas, 2017; Campbell & Gross, 2008). In addition, past research suggests charter principals have less training and experience (Battle, 2009) and tend to have shorter tenures at their schools than traditional principals (Ni, Sun, & Rorrer, 2014).

Noting the unique tasks and complexity faced by charter principals, Mavrogordato, Goldring, and Smrekar (chapter 1) and Reid (chapter 3) suggest charter principals need further training and development than currently provided and required of them to deal with these complexities. As Mavrogordato and colleagues suggest, "charter school principals might need to develop the knowledge and skills around important domains of leadership that are not typically emphasized in traditional leadership programs."

Charter Leadership in Stand-alone versus Networked Charters

Training and development of charter principals may also need to be differentiated by the type of charter school in which the principal works. Charter principals may lead in stand-alone or networked schools, or schools managed by a charter management company (CMO). The authors of three chapters in this text compared how principals from stand-alone charters, networked schools, and CMOs dealt with issues of accountability, teacher evaluation, and succession and socialization of principals. In each case, the authors noted a difference in how principals processed and enacted their leadership depending on whether they were leading a stand-alone school or schools grouped through networking or CMOs.

Mavrogordato and colleagues (chapter 1) determined that principals in stand-alone schools had greater autonomy but less support. Reid (chapter 3) indicated that the stand-alone principal was able to choose which evaluation system he used and how he would implement it. Alternately, the CMO chose the evaluation system for the principal, but allowed discretion regarding how it might be implemented. Gawlik (chapter 5) found that the CMO actually had a formal socialization and succession process compared to no structured process in the stand-alone schools. Although Miranda and Felber-Smith (chapter 2) did not include a CMO principal in their research, they proposed that future research needs to examine more specifically the variations in principals' leadership between stand-alone organizations and CMOs.

IMPLICATIONS FOR PRACTICE

Each chapter in this book builds upon and extends the limited research highlighting the work of the charter principal. The research presented in this book is descriptive and grounded in a variety of contexts. The findings introduce principal leadership issues in charter schools that have yet to be fully explored, specifically accountability demand, teacher evaluation and development, and planning for principal succession and socialization. These qualitative descriptions allow charter principals, as well as traditional principals, to compare and contrast how they deal with these specific leadership issues in contexts similar to their own.

The research reported in this book suggests important questions for those supporting charter principals, such as boards, management organization, and state organizations. Authors clearly outlined that charter principal leadership is complex, and recommend increased preparation and development of charter principals for their work.

Who should provide more formal preparation and professional development to charter principals so that they can more effectively engage in the unique leadership issues of charter schools? What structures should be implemented so that principals are supported as they transition to new positions? How can those responsible for effective charter schooling ease tensions among policy, principal autonomy, and school mission and vision?

Researchers in these chapters have only scratched the surface of the potential principal leadership issues, topics, and skills that might be examined within the charter context. Researchers can explore a plethora of specific topics that may provide charter principals with ideas and solutions to better lead in a context that is different from that faced by the traditional principal.

Researchers, however, may be best served by employing traditional principal leadership frameworks, such as the National Policy Board for Educational Administration's Professional Standards for Educational Leaders, to organize future research. These frameworks might help consolidate the many issues and skills that are required of charter principals and provide direct comparisons to traditional principal leadership.

Researchers should continue to examine how principal autonomy interacts with specific principal practices, as autonomy appears to be pivotal to understanding the differences between how traditional and charter principals engage in leadership. Charter principal autonomy should also be explored in relationship to various charter governance structures. The researchers in this volume suggest that principals in CMOs engage in leadership differently than those in stand-alone charters. There seems to be a trade-off between autonomy given and support provided, with CMOs providing greater support but allowing less autonomy. More research is needed to tease out the characteristics of this continuum.

Although charter policy writ large has been the subject of much of the research related to charter schools (Weitzel & Lubienski, 2010), authors in this text questioned how principals interpreted and implemented policy at the school level. Policy makers should be cognizant of how charter principals use their autonomy to adapt and adjust policy in relationship to intended policy outcomes. The tension between principal autonomy and accountability to policy intentions, although initially examined in this text, should be a topic for further consideration by policy makers, those tasked with monitoring policy implementation, and researchers.

The authors of these chapters provide glimpses into issues faced by charter school principals. They also introduced and expanded on themes that provide insights into how charter school principals engage in their work. We encourage charter principals, charter organizations, researchers, and policy makers to examine their own practices in relationship to these findings. It is our hope that the research presented in this two-book series describing how charter school principals engage in the real work of leadership will prompt further dialogue and action in support of the growing number of charter school principals who lead schools that educate over 2.5 million students in the United States.

Appendix A

Relevant Excerpts from the Principal Interview Protocol

PROFESSIONAL BACKGROUND

1. Where (what school) did you start your career in education? What year?
2. How long have you been an administrator? In what school(s)?
3. What attracted you to a charter school?
4. Why did you choose *this* charter school?

TEACHING AND LEARNING ENVIRONMENT

1. When I walk through the school, will I know this is a *charter* school? What is different or unique?
2. How would you describe the teaching (and learning) philosophy here? What did the charter school founder(s) have in mind originally?
3. How similar or different is this school from a traditional public school in terms of curriculum and instruction (or the organization of teaching and learning)?
4. How are curricular goals and specific instructional content determined? In other words, who decides what teachers teach, and how they teach it?
5. Do teachers have any degrees of "freedom" or "autonomy" here, or is curriculum and instruction (somewhat, moderately, highly) structured?
6. Is your school part of a CMO/EMO? If so, to what degree does your school reflect this model? How, if at all, does this charter school

model shape your decisions as an administrator? Probe for degrees of discretion (to adapt to local context and conditions).
7. As an administrator at this school, do you have any additional financial or material resources at your disposal (external grants, donated equipment)?
8. What are some key funding priorities (how do you allocate these funds: professional development, new equipment, additional facilities)?

GOVERNANCE AND ACCOUNTABILITY

1. How would you compare being an administrator at a charter school to being an administrator at a traditional public school?
2. How would you describe the way in which decisions are made at this school?
3. What role does the teachers' union play at the school? What are some key priority issues for the union?
4. Accountability is often associated with the vision of charter schools. How is accountability defined at your school? What measures are used?
5. In your opinion, who monitors/enforces this accountability (e.g., state, district, CMO/EMO, parents)?

TEACHER RECRUITMENT, RETENTION, AND EVALUATION

1. Do you recruit teachers? How? What qualities do you look as you recruit?
2. Teacher burnout is an issue in both charter schools and traditional public schools. Does your school do anything to address this issue? What?
3. How are teachers' salaries determined? How do salaries compare to traditional public schools?
4. Do you use student assessments to evaluate teacher performance?
5. Are there teacher performance incentives here? If so, what outcome measures are used?

FINAL ADMINISTRATOR QUESTIONS

1. What changes—if any—have you observed at this school since the first year you were an administrator?
2. Have any school policies or priorities shifted since you started here (instruction/academic focus, resources, student population)?

Appendix B

Analytic Approach

Data analyses sought to understand each principal's autonomy in their roles as charter school leaders, and to unpack how they balance this autonomy with state accountability demands. To explore the research questions, we developed an a priori coding framework derived from the interview guide. We applied this framework during our first round of data coding. For example, we coded for examples of autonomy, conditions that allow for autonomy, conditions that constrain autonomy, and accountability demands.

As we coded, new categories and themes emerged, and they were added to the framework (Miles & Huberman, 1994). We used this strategy of coding and thematic analysis to reveal patterns among the principals. Repeated analyses of the interview transcripts allowed for more fine-grained coding to take place within each of the baseline nodes, and additional nodes emerged and were added to the analysis framework. The analyses include thick, rich descriptions of the patterns and themes that emerged from the data.

References

Ableidinger, J., & Hassel, B. C. (2010). *Free to lead: Autonomy in highly successful charter schools*. Washington, DC: National Alliance for Public Charter Schools.
Allen, J., & Consoletti, A. (2010). *Annual survey of America's charter schools*. Washington, DC: Center for Education Reform. Retrieved from https://www.edreform.com/wp-content/uploads/2011/09/CER_Charter_Survey_2010.pdf
Apple, M. (1996). *Cultural Politics and Education.* New York: Teachers College Press.
Apple, M. (2001). *Educating the "right" way: Markets, standards, God and inequality.* New York: Routledge Falmer.
Arsen, D., Plank, D., & Sykes, G. (1999). *School choice policies in Michigan: The rules matter.* East Lansing, MI: School Choice and Educational Change, Michigan State University.
Barghaus, K. M., & Boe, E. E. (2011). From policy to practice: Implementation of the legislative objectives of charter schools. *American Journal of Education, 118*(1), 57–86.
Battle, D. (2009). Characteristics of public, private, and Bureau of Indian Education elementary and secondary school principals in the United States: Results from the 2007–08 Schools and Staffing Survey (NCES 2009-323). Retrieved from http://nces.ed.gov/pubs2009/2009323.pdf
Bengtson, E., Zepeda, S. J., & Parylo, O. (2013). School systems' practices of controlling socialization during principal succession: Looking through the lens of organizational socialization theory. *Journal of Educational Administration, 41*(2): 143–164.
Berends, M. (2015). Sociology and school choice: What we know after two decades of charter schools. *Annual Review of Sociology, 41*, 159–180.
Berends, M., Goldring, E., Stein, M., & Cravens, X. (2010). Instructional conditions in charter schools and students' mathematics achievement gains. *American Journal of Education, 116*(3), 303–335.
Berg, B. L. (2007). *Qualitative research methods for the social sciences* (6th ed.). San Francisco: Pearson Education.
Berman, P., & McLaughlin, M. W. (1978). *Federal programs supporting educational change, vol. 8: Implementing and sustaining innovations.* Santa Monica, CA: Rand Corporation.
Bickmore, D. L., & Gawlik, M. A. (Eds.). (2017). *The Charter School Principal: Nuanced Descriptions of Leadership*. Lanham, MD: Rowman & Littlefield.
Bickmore, D. L., & Dowell, M. M. (2011). Concerns, use of time, and the intersection of leadership: Case study of two charter school principals. *Research in Schools, 18*(1), 44–61.
Bickmore, D. L., & Dowell, M. (2014). Two Charter School Principals' Engagement in Instructional Leadership. *Journal of School Leadership, 24*(5), 842–881.
Bidwell, C. E. (2001). Analyzing schools as organizations: Long-term permanence and short-term change. *Sociology of Education, 74*(5), 100–114.

References

Black, P., & Wiliam, D. (1998). Assessment and classroom learning. *Assessment in Education: Principles, Policy & Practice, 5*(1), 7–74.

Blasé, R., Blasé, J., & Phillips, D. Y. (2010). *Handbook of school improvement: How high-performing principals create high-performing schools.* Thousand Oaks, CA: Corwin Press.

Boris-Schacter, S., & Langer, S. (2002). Caught between nostalgia and utopia. *Education Week, 21* (February 6): 34, 36–37.

Boyd, D., Grossman, P., Ing, M., Lankford, H., & Wyckoff, J. (2011). The influence of school administrators on teacher retention decisions. *American Educational Research Journal, 48*(2), 303–333.

Briggs, A. R., Bush, T., & Middlewood, D. (2006). From immersion to establishment: The challenges facing new school heads and the role of "new visions" in resolving them. *Cambridge Journal of Education, 36*(2): 257–276.

Browne-Ferrigno, T. (2003). Becoming a principal: Role conception, initial socialization, professional development, and capacity building. *Education Administration Quarterly, 40*(4), 389–407.

Buddin, R., & Zimmer, R. (2005). Student achievement in charter schools: A complex picture. *Journal of Policy Analysis and Management, 24*(2), 351–371.

Bulkley, K. E. (2004). Reinventing an Idea: The political construction of charter schools. *Educational Foundations, 18*(1), 5–31.

Bulkley, K. E., & Wohlstetter, P. (Eds.). (2004). *Taking account of charter schools: What's happened and what's next?* New York: Teachers College Press.

Bush, T., & Oduro, G. K. (2006). New Principals in Africa: Preparation, induction and practice. *Journal of Educational Administration, 44*(4): 359–375.

Buunk, A. P., & Gibbons, F. X. (2007). Social comparison: The end of a theory and the emergence of a field. *Organizational Behavior and Human Decision Processes, 102*(1), 3–21.

California Commission on Teacher Credentialing (2009). *California standards for the teaching profession.* Retrieved from http://www.ctc.ca.gov/educator-prep/standards/CSTP-2009.pdf

Cambron-McCabe, N., & McCarthy, M. M. (2005). Educating school principals for social justice. *Educational Policy, 19*(1), 201–222.

Campbell, C. (2010). *You're leaving?: Succession and sustainability in charter schools.* Seattle: Center on Reinventing Public Education, University of Washington.

Campbell, C., & Gross, B. (2008). *Working without a safety net: How charter school leaders can best survive on the high wire.* Seattle: National Charter School Research Project, Center on Reinventing Public Education, University of Washington.

Campbell, C., Gross, B., & Lake, R. (2008). The high-wire job of charter school leadership. *Education Week, 28*(3), S6–S8.

Campbell, C., & Grubb, B. J. (2008). *Closing the skill gap: New options for charter school leadership development.* Seattle: National Charter School Research Project, Center on Reinventing Public Education, University of Washington. Retrieved from http://www.crpe.org/sites/default/files/pub_ncsrp_icslead_aug14_0.pdf

Cannata, M., & Engel, M. (2012). Does charter status determine preferences?: Comparing the hiring preferences of charter and traditional public school principals. *Education, 7*(4), 455–488.

Cannata, M., Thombre, Z., & Thomas, G. (2017). The first principal: Perspectives on founding a charter school. In D. L. Bickmore & M. A. Gawlik (Eds.), *The Charter School Principal: Nuanced Descriptions of Leadership.* Lanham, MD: Rowman & Littlefield.

Center for American Progress. (2009). *Aligned by design: How teacher compensation reform can support and reinforce other educational reforms.* Washington DC: Center for American Progress.

Center for Education Reform. (2014).*Charter school facts.* Retrieved from http://www.edreform.com/

Center for Public Education. (2013). *Trends in teacher evaluation.* Retrieved from http://www.centerforpubliceducation.org/Main-Menu/Evaluating-performance/

Chetty, R., Friedman, J. N., & Rockoff, J. E. (2014). Measuring the impacts of teachers II: Teacher value-added and student outcomes in adulthood. *American Economic Review, 104*(9), 2633–2679.

Chubb, J. E., & Moe, T. M. (1990). *Politics, markets and America's schools.* Washington, DC: Brookings Institution.

Clandinin, D. J., Kennedy, M., Rocque, L. L., & Pearce, M. (1996). Living the tension: A case study of teacher stories of teacher evaluation. *Journal of Education Policy, 11*(2), 169–183.

Coburn, C. E. (2005). Shaping teacher sensemaking: School leaders and the enactment of reading policy. *Educational Policy, 19*(3), 476–509.

Cowie, M., & Crawford, M. (2008). "Being" a new principal in Scotland. *Journal of Educational Administration, 46*(6): 676–689.

Cravens, X., Goldring, E., & Peñaloza, R. (2009). *Leadership practices and school choice.* Paper presented at the American Educational Research Association Annual Conference, San Diego, CA.

Creswell, J. W. (2014). *Research design: Qualitative, quantitative, and mixed methods approaches* (4th ed.). Thousand Oaks, CA: Sage.

Crow, G. M. (2006). Complexity and the beginning principal in the United States: Perspectives on socialization. *Journal of Educational Administration, 44*(4), 310–325.

Danielson, C. (2007). *Enhancing professional practice: a framework for teaching* (2nd ed.). Alexandria, VA: Association for Supervision and Curriculum Development.

Danielson, C. (2011). Evaluations that help teachers learn. *Educational Leadership, 68*(4), 35–39.

Danielson, C., & McGreal, T. (2000). *Teacher evaluation to enhance professional practice.* Alexandria, VA: Association for Supervision and Curriculum Development.

Darling-Hammond, L. (2013). *Getting teacher evaluation right: What really matters for effectiveness and improvement.* New York: Teachers College Press.

Darling-Hammond, L., Wise, A., & Pease, S. (1983). Teacher evaluation in the organizational context: A review of the literature. *Review of Educational Research, 53*(3), 285–328.

Datnow, A., Hubbard, L., & Mehan, H. (2002). *Extending educational reform: From one school to many*. London: Routledge Falmer.

Davis, D. R., Ellett, C. D., & Annunziata, J. (2002). Teacher evaluation, leadership and learning organizations. *Journal of Personnel Evaluation in Education, 16*(4), 287–301.

Davis, S., Darling-Hammond, L., LaPointe, M., & Meyerson, D. (2005). *School leadership study: Developing successful principals.* Stanford, CA: Stanford Educational Leadership Institute.

Dressler, B. (2001). Charter school leadership. *Education and Urban Society, 33*(2), 170–185.

Duke, D. L., & Stiggins, R. J. (1986). *Teacher evaluation: Five keys to growth.* Washington, DC: National Educational Association.

Duke, D. L., & Stiggins, R. J. (1990). Beyond minimum competence: Evaluation for professional development. In J. Millman & L. Darling-Hammond (Eds.), *The new handbook of teacher evaluation: Assessing elementary and secondary school teachers,* (pp. 116–132). Newbury Park, CA: Corwin Press.

Elmore, R. F. (2004). *School reform from the inside out: Policy, practice, and performance.* Cambridge, MA: Harvard Education.

Erlandson, D., Harris, E., Skipper, B., and Allen, S. (1993). *Doing naturalistic inquiry: A guide to methods.* Newbury Park, CA: Sage.

Farrell, C., Nayfack, M. B., Smith, J., & Wohlstetter, P. (2014). One size does not fit all: Understanding the variation in charter management scale-up. *Journal of Educational Change, 15*(1), 77–97.

Farrell, C., Wohlstetter, P., & Smith, J. (2012). Charter management organizations: An emerging approach to scaling up what works. *Educational Policy, 26*(4), 499–532.

Fink, D., & Brayman, C. (2004). Principals' succession and educational change. *Journal of Educational Administration, 42*(4), 431–39.

Fink, D., & Brayman, C. (2006). School principalship succession and the challenges of change. *Educational Administration Quarterly, 42*(1), 62–89.

Finnigan, K. S. (2007). Charter school autonomy: The mismatch between theory and practice. *Educational Policy, 21*(3), 503–526.

Florida Department of Education. (2015). Charter Schools FAQs. Retrieved from http://www.fldoe.org/schools/school-choice/charter-schools/charter-school-faqs.stml

Fuller, B. (2000). *Inside charter schools: The paradox of radical decentralization.* Cambridge, MA: Harvard University Press.

Fuller, E., & Young, M. (2009). *Tenure and retention of newly hired principals in Texas.* Austin: University Council of Educational Administration, University of Texas.

Gawlik, M. A. (2007). Beyond the charter school house door: Teacher perceived autonomy. *Education and Urban Society, 39*(4), 524–553.

Gawlik, M. A. (2008). Breaking loose: Principal autonomy in charter and public schools. *Educational Policy, 22*(6), 783–804.

Gawlik, M. A. (2012). Moving beyond the rhetoric: Charter school reform and accountability. *Journal of Educational Research, 105*(3), 210–219.

Gawlik, M. A. (2015). Shared sense-making: How charter school leaders ascribe meaning to accountability. *Journal of Educational Administration, 53*(3), 393–415.

Gawlik, M. A. (2016). The U.S. charter school landscape: Extant literature, gaps in research, and implications for the U.S. educational system. *Global Education Review, 3*(2), 50–83.

Glaser, B. G. (1965). The constant comparative method of qualitative analysis. *Social Problems, 12*(4), 436–445.

Glaser, B. G., & Strauss, A. (1967). *The discovery of grounded theory: Strategies for qualitative research.* Chicago: Aldine Publishing Co.

Goddard, R. D., & Salloum, S. (2011). Collective efficacy beliefs, organizational excellence, and leadership. In K. Cameron & G. Spreitzer (Eds.), *Positive organizational scholarship handbook,* (pp. 642–650). Oxford: Oxford University Press.

Goff, P. T., Mavrogordato, M., & Goldring, E. (2012). Instructional leadership in charter schools: Is there an organizational effect or are leadership practices the result of faculty characteristics and preferences? *Leadership and Policy in Schools, 11*(1), 1–25.

Goldring, E., Grissom, J. A., Ruben, M., Neumerski, C. M., Cannata, M., Drake, T., & Schuermann, P. (2015). Make room value added: Principals' human capital decisions and the emergence of teacher observation data. *Educational Researcher, 44*(2), 96–104.

Goldring, E., & Mavrogordato, M. (2011). International perspectives on academies: Lessons learned from charter schools and choice options around the globe. In H. M. Gunter (Ed.), *The state and education policy: The academies programme,* (pp. 185–198). London: Continuum.

Grissom, J. A., & Loeb, S. (forthcoming). Assessing principals' assessments: Subjective evaluations of teacher effectiveness in low- and high-stakes environments. *Education Finance and Policy.*

Gross, B. (2011). *Inside charter schools: Unlocking doors to student success.* Seattle: Center on Reinventing Public Education, University of Washington.

Hallinger, P., Heck, R. H., & Murphy, J. (2014). Teacher evaluation and school improvement: An analysis of the evidence. *Educational Assessment, Evaluation and Accountability, 26*(1), 5–28.

Halverson, R., & Clifford, M. (2006). Evaluation in the wild: A distributed cognitive perspective on teacher assessment. *Educational Administration Quarterly, 42*(4), 578–619.

Halverson, R., Kelley, C., & Kimball, S. (2004). Implementing teacher evaluation systems: How principals make sense of complex artifacts to shape local instructional practice. In C. Miskel & W. Hoy (Eds.), *Theory and research in educational administration,* (pp. 66–90). Greenwich, CT: Information Age Press.

Hannan, M. T., & Freeman, J. (1984). Structural inertia and organizational change. *American Sociological Review, 49*(2), pp. 149–164.

Hanushek, E. A., & Rivkin, S. G. (2010). Generalizations about using value-added measures of teacher quality. *American Economic Review, 100*(2), 267–271.

Hargreaves, A. & Fink, D. (2006). *Sustainable Principalship.* San Francisco: Jossey-Bass.

Hargreaves, A., Moore, S., Fink, D., Brayman, C., & White, R. (2003). *Succeeding Principals: A study of principal succession and sustainability.* Boston: Boston College.

References

Harlen, W., & James, M. (1997). Assessment and learning: Differences and relationships between formative and summative assessment. *Assessment in Education, 4*(3), 365–379.

Harris, D. N., Rutledge, S. A., Ingle, W. K., & Thompson, C. C. (2010). Mix and match: What principals really look for when hiring teachers. *Education Finance and Policy, 5*(2), 228–246.

Hart, A. (1993). *Principal Succession: Establishing Leadership in Schools.* Albany: State University of New York Press.

Hausman, C., & Goldring, E. (2001). Sustaining teacher commitment: The role of professional communities. *Peabody Journal of Education, 76*(2), 30–51.

Hill, H., & Grossman, P. (2013). Learning from teacher observations: Challenges and opportunities posed by new teacher evaluation systems. *Harvard Educational Review, 83*(2), 371–384.

Honig, M. I., & Hatch, T. C. (2004). Crafting coherence: How schools strategically manage multiple, external demands. *Educational Researcher, 33*(8), 16–30.

Hoy, W. K., & Miskel, C. G. (2008). *Educational administration: Theory, research, and practice (8th ed.).* New York: McGraw-Hill.

Hull, J. (2012). *The principal perspective: Full report.* Retrieved from http://www.centerforpubliceducation.org/principal-perspective

Jacob, B. A. (2011). Do principals fire the worst teachers? *Educational Evaluation and Policy Analysis, 33*(4), 403–434.

Kimball, S. (2002). Analysis of feedback, enabling conditions, and fairness perceptions of teachers in three school districts with new standards-based evaluation systems. *Journal of Personnel Evaluation in Education, 16*(4), 241–268.

Knapp, M. S., Copland, M. A., Plecki, M. L., & Portin, B. S. (2006). *Leading, learning, and leadership support.* Seattle: Center for the Study of Teaching and Policy, University of Washington. Retrieved from https://depts.washington.edu/ctpmail/PDFs/Synthesis-Oct16.pdf

Kraft, M. A., & Gilmour, A. F. (2015). *Can principals promote teacher development as evaluators?: A 21 case study of principals' views and experiences.* Providence, RI: Brown University Working Papers.

Ladd, H. F. (2011). Teachers' perceptions of their working conditions. *Educational Evaluation and Policy Analysis, 33*(2), 235–261. doi:10.3102/0162373711398128

Lake, R., Dusseault, B., Bowen, M., Demeritt, A., & Hill, P. (2010). *The national study of charter management organization (CMO) effectiveness: Report on interim findings.* Seattle, WA: Mathematical Policy Research, Inc., and Center on Reinventing Public Education.

Leithwood, K., Harris, A., & Hopkins, D. (2008). Seven strong claims about successful school leadership. *School Leadership & Management, 28*(1), 27–42.

Leithwood, K., Patten, S., & Jantzi, D. (2010). Testing a conception of how school leadership influences student learning. *Educational Administration Quarterly, 46*(5), 671–706.

Leithwood, K., Seashore-Louis, K., Anderson, S., & Wahlstrom, K. (2004). *How leadership influences student learning.* New York: The Wallace Foundation. Retrieved from http://www.wallacefoundation.org/knowledge-center/Pages/How-Leadership-Influences-Student-Learning.aspx

Lincoln, Y. S., & Guba, E. G. (1985). *Naturalistic inquiry.* Beverly Hills, CA: Sage.

Loeb, S., Kalogrides, D., & Horng, E. (2010). Principal preferences and the uneven distribution of principals across schools. *Educational Evaluation and Policy Analysis, 32*(2), 205–229.

Louis, K. S., Leithwood, K., Wahlstrom, K. L. & Anderson, S. E. (2010). *Learning from leadership project: Investigating the links to improved student learning.* Minneapolis: Center for Applied Research and Educational Improvement, University of Minnesota, and Toronto: Ontario Institute for Studies in Education, University of Toronto. Retrieved from http://www.wallacefoundation.org/knowledge-center/Documents/Investigating-the-Links-to-Improved-Student-Learning.pdf

Louis, K. S., & Robinson, V. M. (2012). External mandates and instructional leadership: school leaders as mediating agents. *Journal of Educational Administration, 50*(5), 629–665.

Lubienski, C. (2003). Innovation in education markets: Theory and evidence on the impact of competition and choice in charter schools. *American Educational Research Journal, 40*(2), 395–443.

Lubienski, C. (2004). Charter school innovation in theory and practice: Autonomy, R&D, and curricular conformity. In K. E. Bulkley & P. Wohlstetter (Eds.), *Taking account of charter schools: What's happened and what's next,* (pp. 72–90). New York: Teachers College Press.

Lubienski, C. (2006). School diversification in second-best education markets: International evidence and conflicting theories of change. *Educational Policy, 20*(2), 323–344.

Malen, B., Rice, J. K., Matlach, L. K., Bowsher, A., Hoyer, K. M., & Hyde, L. H. (2015). Developing organizational capacity for implementing complex education reform initiatives: Insights from a multiyear study of a Teacher Incentive Fund Program. *Educational Administration Quarterly, 51*(1), 133–176.

Marsh, J., Springer, M., McCaffrey, F., Yuan, K., Epstein, S., Koppich, et al. (2011). *A big apple for educators: New York City's experiment with schoolwide performance bonuses.* Santa Monica, CA: Rand Corporation.

Max, K., Constantine, J., Wellington, A., Halgren, K., Glazeman, S., Chiang, S., et al. (2014). Evaluation of the Teacher Incentive Fund: Implementation and early impacts of pay-for-performance after one year. Retrieved from the ERIC database, http://files.eric.ed.gov/fulltext/ED546820.pdf

McLaughlin, M. W., & Talbert, J. E. (1993). *Contexts that matter for teaching and learning: Strategic opportunities for meeting the nation's educational goals.* Washington, DC: Center for Research on the Context of Secondary School Teaching.

Merseth, K. K. (2009). *Inside urban charter schools: Promising practices and strategies in five high-performing schools.* Cambridge, MA: Harvard Education Publishing Group.

Milanowski, A., & Heneman III, H. (2001). Assessment of teacher reactions to a standards-based teacher evaluation system: A pilot study. *Journal of Personnel Evaluation in Education, 15*(3), 193–212.

Milanowski, A., Witham, P., Schuermann, P., Kimball, S., & Pietryka, D. (2010). *Harvesting lessons on educator incentive plan design from technical assistance provided to Teacher Incentive Fund grants.* Paper presented at the annual meeting of the American Educational Finance Association, Richmond, VA.

Miles, M., & Huberman, A. (1994). *Qualitative data analysis.* Thousand Oaks, CA: Sage.

Miles, M., Huberman, A., & Saldaña, J. (2014). *Qualitative data analysis: A methods sourcebook* (3rd ed.). Thousand Oaks, CA: Sage.

Millman, J., & Darling-Hammond, L. (1990). *The new handbook of teacher evaluation: Assessing elementary and secondary school teachers.* London: Sage Publications.

Minnesota Department of Education. (2016). *Q-Comp Application Guidelines.* Retrieved from http://education.state.mn.us/MDE/dse/qc/

Miron, G., & Applegate, B. (2007). *Teacher attrition in charter schools.* Tempe, AZ: Education Policy Research Unit, and Boulder, CO: Education and the Public Interest Center. Retrieved from http://greatlakescenter.org/docs/Research/Miron_Attrition.pdf

Miron, G., & Nelson, C. (2002). *What's public about charter schools?: Lessons learned about choice and accountability.* Thousand Oaks, CA: Corwin Press.

Miskel, C., & Cosgrove, D. (1985). Leader succession in school settings. *Review of Educational Research, 55*(1), 87–105.

Murphy, J., Hallinger, P., & Heck, R. H. (2013). Leading via teacher evaluation: The case of the missing clothes? *Educational Researcher, 42*(6), 349–354.

National Alliance for Public Charter Schools. (2013). *Charter school data dashboard: Florida.* Retrieved from http://dashboard2.publiccharters.org/State/?state=FL

National Alliance for Public Charter Schools. (2014). *The public charter schools dashboard.* Retrieved from http://www.publiccharters.org/dashboard/home

National Alliance for Public Charter Schools. (2015). *Measuring up: A tool for comparing state charter school laws and movements.* Retrieved from http://www.publiccharters.org/get-the-facts/law-database

Nelson, S. W., de la Colina, M. G., & Boone, M. D. (2008). Lifeworld or systemworld: What guides novice principals. *Journal of Educational Administration, 46*(6): 690–701.

References

Ni, Y., Sun, M., & Rorrer, A. (2014). Principal turnover: Upheaval and uncertainty in charter schools? *Educational Administration Quarterly, 51*(3), 1–29. doi:10.1177/0013161X14539808

Normore, A. H. (2004). Socializing school administrators to meet leadership challenges that doom all but the most heroic and talented leaders to fail. *International Journal of Leadership in Education, 7*(2): 107–125.

Oberfield, Z. W. (2016). A bargain half fulfilled: Teacher autonomy and accountability in traditional public schools and public charter schools. *American Educational Research Journal*, Advance online publication. doi:10.3102/0002831216634843

Odell, S. J. (1997). Preparing teachers for teacher leadership. *Action in Teacher Education, 19*(3), 120–124.

Patton, M. Q. (1990). *Qualitative evaluation methods* (2nd ed.). Thousand Oaks, CA: Sage.

Pianta, R. C., & Hamre, B. K. (2009). Conceptualization, measurement, and improvement of classroom processes: Standardized observation can leverage capacity. *Educational Researcher, 38*(2), 109–119.

Podgursky, M. J. (2006). Teams versus bureaucracies: Personnel policy, wage-setting, and teacher quality in traditional public, charter, and private schools. Retrieved from ERIC database, https://eric.ed.gov/?id=ED509018

Podgursky, M. J. (2008). *Market-Based Pay Reform for Public School Teachers.* Nashville, TN: National Center on Performance Incentives. Retrieved from https://my.vanderbilt.edu/performanceincentives/files/2012/10/200807_Podgursky_MarketBasedPay1.pdf

Podgursky, M. J., & Springer, M. G. (2007). Teacher performance pay: A review. *Journal of Policy Analysis and Management, 26*(4), 909–950.

Popham, W. J. (1988). The dysfunctional marriage of formative and summative teacher evaluation. *Journal of Personnel Evaluation in Education, 1*(3), 269–273.

Portin, B., Schneider, P., DeArmond, M., & Gundlach, L. (2003). *Making sense of leading schools: A study of the school principalship.* Seattle: Center on Reinventing Public Education.

Pounder, D. G., & Merrill, R. J. (2001). Job desirability of the high school principalship: A job choice theory perspective. *Educational Administration Quarterly, 37*(1), 27–57.

Preston, C., Goldring, E., Berends, M., & Cannata, M. (2012). School innovation in district context: Comparing traditional public schools and charter schools. *Economics of Education Review, 31*(2), 318–330.

Rice, J. K., Malen, B., Baumann, P., Chen, E., Dougherty, A., Hyde, L., et al. (2012). The persistent problems and confounding challenges of educator incentives: The case of TIF in Prince George's County, Maryland. *Educational Policy, 26*(6), 892–933.

Richert, C. (2011).Polygraph: Pawlenty tells part of the story on teacher pay. *Minnesota Public Radio*, April 22. Retrieved from http://blogs.mprnews.org/capitol-view/2011/04/poligraph_1/

Rigby, J. (2015). Principals' sensemaking and enactment of teacher evaluation. *Journal of Educational Administration, 53*(3), 374–392.

Robinson, V. M., Lloyd, C. A., & Rowe, K. J. (2008). The impact of leadership on student outcomes: An analysis of the differential effects of leadership types. *Educational Administration Quarterly, 44*(5), 635–674.

Rockoff, J. E. (2004). The impact of individual teachers on student achievement: Evidence from panel data. *American Economic Review, 94*(2), 247–252.

Smylie, M. A. (2010). *Continuous school improvement.* Thousand Oaks, CA: Corwin Press.

Smylie, M. A., Conley, S., & Marks, H. M. (2002). Exploring new approaches to teacher leadership for school improvement. In J. Murphy (Ed.), *The educational leadership challenge: Redefining leadership for the 21st century* (pp. 162–188). Chicago: University of Chicago Press.

Speakman, S. T. (2008). Back to the future: Sustaining an equitable public-private model of school funding. In M. Berends, M. G. Springer, & H. J. Walberg (Eds.), *Charter school outcomes* (pp. 85–112). New York: Lawrence Erlbaum Associates.

Spillane, J. P. (1998). State policy and the non-monolithic nature of the local school district: Organizational and professional considerations. *American Educational Research Journal, 35*(1), 33–63.

Spillane, J. P. (2000). Cognition and policy implementation: District policymakers and the reform of mathematics education. *Cognition and Instruction, 18*(2), 141–179.

Spillane, J. P., Diamond, J. B., Burch, P., Hallett, T., Jita, L., & Zoltners, J. (2002). Managing in the middle: School leaders and the enactment of accountability policy. *Educational Policy, 16*(5), 731–762.

Spillane, J. P., Reiser, B. J., & Reimer, T. (2002). Policy implementation and cognition: Reframing and refocusing implementation research. *Review of Educational Research, 72*(3), 387–431.

Stuit, D. A., & Smith, T. M. (2010). *Teacher turnover in charter schools: Research brief.* Nashville, TN: National Center on School Choice, Vanderbilt University.

Stuit, D. A., & Smith, T. M. (2012). Explaining the gap in charter and traditional public school teacher turnover rates. *Economics of Education Review, 31*(2), 268–279.

Taras, M. (2005). Assessment: Summative and formative: Some theoretical reflections. *British Journal of Educational Studies, 53*(4), 466–478.

Timperley, H., & Robinson, V. (1998). Collegiality in schools: Its nature and implications for problem solving. *Education Administration Quarterly, 34*(Supplemental), 608–629.

Triant, B. (2001) *Autonomy and innovation: How do Massachusetts charter school principals use their freedom?* Washington, DC: Thomas B. Fordham Institute.

Trujillo, T. (2013). The disproportionate erosion of local control: Urban school boards, high-stakes accountability, and democracy. *Educational Policy, 27*(2), 334–359.

Tucker, P. (1997). Lake Wobegon: Where all teachers are competent (or, have we come to terms with the problem of incompetent teachers?). *Journal of Personnel Evaluation in Education, 11*(2), 103–126.

U.S. Census Bureau (2012). *Population estimates.* Retrieved from www.census.gov

U.S. Department of Education. (2009). *Race to the Top program executive summary.* Retrieved from http://www2.ed.gov/programs/racetothetop/executive-summary.pdf

U.S. Department of Education (2016). *Teacher Incentive Fund.* Retrieved from http://www2.ed.gov/programs/teacherincentive/index.html

Van Maanen, J., & Schein, E. H. (1979). Toward a theory of organizational socialization. In B. M. Staw (Ed.), *Research in organizational behavior, vol. 1: Annual series of analytical essays and critical reviews,* 209–309. Greenwich, CT: JAI Press.

Wahlstrom, K., Seashore, K., Leithwood, K., & Anderson, S. (2010). *Investigating the links to improved student learning: Executive summary of research findings.* Minneapolis: Center for Applied Research and Educational Improvement, University of Minnesota.

Wahlstrom, K., Sheldon, T., & Peterson, K. (2006). *Implementation of the Quality Compensation program (Q-Comp): A formative evaluation.* Minneapolis: Center for Applied Research and Educational Improvement, University of Minnesota.

Walberg, H. J., & Bast, J. L. (2003). *Education and capitalism: How overcoming our fear of markets and economics can improve America's schools.* Stanford, CA: Hoover Institution Press.

Walker, A. & Qian, H. (2006). Beginning principals: Balancing at the top of the greasy pole. *Journal of Educational Administration, 44*(4): 297–309.

Weatherly, R., & Lipsky, M. (1977). Street-level bureaucrats and institutional innovation: Implementing special education reform. *Harvard Educational Review, 47*(2), 171–197.

Weindling, D. (2000). *Stages of headship: A longitudinal study of the principalship.* Paper presented at the American Educational Research Association, New Orleans.

Weisberg, D., Sexton, S., Mulhern, J., & Keeling, D. (2009). *The widget effect: Our national failure to acknowledge and act on differences in teacher effectiveness.* New York: The New Teacher Project.

Weitzel, P. C. , & Lubienski, C. A. (2010). Grading charter schools: Access, innovation, and competition. In C. A. Lubienski & P. C. Weitzel (Eds.), *The charter school experiment: Expectations, evidence, and implications* (pp. 15–32). Cambridge, MA: Harvard Education Press.

Wells, A. S., Grutzik, C., Carnochan, S., Slayton, J., & Vasudeva, A. (1999). Underlying policy assumptions of charter school reform: The multiple meanings of a movement. *Teachers College Record, 100*(3), 513–535.

Wise, A. E., Darling-Hammond L., McLaughlin, M. W., & Berstein, H. T. (1985). Teacher evaluation: A study of effective practices. *Elementary School Journal 86*(1), 60–121.

Wohlstetter, P., & Chau, D. (2004). Does autonomy matter?: Implementing research-based practices in charter and other public schools. In K. E. Bulkley & P. Wohlstetter (Eds.), *Taking account of charter schools: What's happened and what's next?* (pp. 53–71). New York: Teachers College Press.

Wohlstetter, P., Malloy, C. L., Hentschke, G., & Smith, J. (2004). Improving service delivery in education through collaboration: An exploratory study of the role of cross-sectoral alliances in the development and support of charter schools. *Social Science Quarterly, 85*(5), 1078–1096.

Wohlstetter, P., Malloy, C. L., Smith, J., & Hentschke, G. (2004). Incentives for charter schools: Building school capacity through cross-sectoral alliances. *Educational Administration Quarterly, 40*(3), 321–365.

Wohlstetter, P., Smith, J., & Farrell, C. (2013). *Choices and challenges: Charter school performance in perspective.* Cambridge, MA: Harvard Education Press.

Wohlstetter, P., Wenning, R., & Briggs, K. L. (1995). Charter schools in the United States: The question of autonomy. *Educational Policy, 9*(4), 331–358.

Wynne, J. (2001) *Teachers as leaders in education reform.* EDO-SP-2001-5. Washington, DC: ERIC Clearinghouse on Teaching and Teacher Education.

Yin, R. (2009). *Case study research: Design and methods* (4th ed.). Thousand Oaks, CA: Sage.

Zimpher, N. L. (1988). A design for professional development of teacher leaders. *Journal of Teacher Education, 39*(1), 53–60.

Index

accountability: autonomy and, viii; charter schools, xi, xvii; principal, 2, 5, 7, 18, 21, 82, 83, 104, 108
Acorn school, 66, 71, 73, 74, 75
Adequate Yearly Progress, 19
affiliated charter schools, 19–20
African American students, 5, 50, 88–89
American Indian students, 30
Annual Performance Index, California's, 71
Asian students, 30
Asian American students, 29, 88, 89
autonomy: accountability and, viii; charter schools and, xi, 1, 2; principals and, xviii, 2, 3–4, 5, 20–21, 81, 103, 104, 106, 107, 108, 109

Board of Trustees, 16–17
bonuses, monetary, 31, 61, 63, 64, 65
Bridge school, 66, 71, 72, 74, 75, 76
budget, 7, 8, 13. *See also* funding
budget management, 3, 12–15, 17

California: Annual Performance Index and, 71; charter schools, xii
California Standards for the Teaching Profession, 63
capacity restraints, 15–16
central office support: charter school, xxi, 23, 42, 82; public school, 42, 44

charter management organization (CMO), vii, 4, 5, 19, 21, 22, 47, 90, 100, 107, 108, 109; teacher evaluation system and, 49, 50
Cohen, Ms., 47, 48, 49, 50, 52
Common Core State Standards, 71
community-based leadership, 93, 94, 99
conversion charter schools, xix
curriculum, 8, 9–10
Cypress school, 66, 69–70, 71, 72, 73, 74, 76

Danielson Framework of Teaching, 48, 49, 50, 64
data collection, Florida charter schools and, 87
data dashboards, performance, 64, 69, 71, 74, 78
Davis Community College, 5, 6, 7, 12. *See also* Jones, Ms.
Dedoose software, 66
Diego Rivera Academy, 27, 29, 38, 39, 40; Q-Comp and, 28, 34–37, 38, 39

education reforms, 43
educational management organization (EMO), vii
educational policy, implementation of, 25–26
English Learner students, 30
Every Student Succeeds Act, 76

125

Expeditionary Learning, 16

facility management, 2
Florida: charter schools, xii, 85–86; data collection, 87. *See also* Purple charter school; Red charter school; White charter school
formative evaluation of teaching (FET), 63, 67, 74
funding, charter school, ix, 1, 2

Gates Foundation, 12
Gatlin School, 5, 6, 12, 18, 19. *See also* Smith, Ms.
goals, school, xii, 31, 35, 38

Hawaii, viii
Hispanic students, 30
human resources, xix–xx, xxi, 6, 7, 8, 10–12

independent charter schools, 19–20, 22, 47
innovation, 1, 9, 66, 81, 98, 105, 107

Jones, Ms., 6, 7, 9, 14, 17

King College Preparatory Academy, 5, 6, 7, 15, 18. *See also* West, Mr.

Laker Charter School, 23, 27, 29, 38, 39, 40; Q-Comp and, 28–34
Latino students, 88–89
leadership team (LT), 34, 37, 38
Loyola Marymount University, 22

mentors, 27, 35, 52, 53–54, 57
Mercer University, 22
Michigan, 46, 50; charter school, xii; teacher evaluation policies in, 46
Michigan Schools Accountability Scorecard, 46, 50
middle class, charter schools and, xvii
Minnesota Department of Education (MDE), 26
Minnesota Quality Compensation Policy. *See* Quality Compensation Policy
mission, school, viii, ix, xii, xviii, 6, 7, 8–9, 10, 12, 18, 20, 21, 104, 105

National Policy Board for Educational Administration, 109
Natural Energy Laboratory of Hawaii, viii
neoconservatives, charter schools and, xvii
neoliberals, charter schools and, xvii
networked charter schools, 107
No Child Left Behind (NCLB), 19, 46

observation: peer, 31, 32, 33, 34, 38; process, 31; rubric, 11, 12, 31, 34, 37, 38, 44

peer: coaching, 30, 31; observation, 31, 32, 33, 34, 38
performance data dashboards, 64, 69, 71, 74, 78
performance evaluation systems, ix
performance management systems, 67, 73, 78–79; Acorn school and, 66; Bridge school, 66; Cypress school, 66, 70, 73; findings, 66; implications of, 78–79; interviews for, 66, 67; methodology, 66; Teacher Incentive Fund and, 61, 62, 63, 64, 69, 70, 76, 77; teachers and, 61; technology requirements, 69; videos and, 63, 69, 78
policy implementation, charter school, 106–107
principal, 44; accountability and, 2, 5, 7, 18, 21, 82, 83, 104, 108; Acorn school, 71; autonomy and, xviii, 2, 3–4, 5, 20–21, 81, 103, 104, 106, 107, 108, 109; Board of Trustees and, 16–17; Bridge school, 71, 72; budget and, 3, 7, 12–13, 14–15, 17, 21; capacity restraints of, 15–16; case study schools, 6; central office support, 82; challenges of, 82; charter management organization and, 90; communication, 96; constraints, 13–17, 104, 106; context-specific concerns, 83; Cypress school, 71; development, 107; duties, xviii; flexibility, 52–53, 55, 56, 57, 58–59, 104, 105, 107; Florida charter schools and, 86, 87; instructional, 82; interviews, 47, 87; Laker Charter School and, 29; leadership, 34, 37, 103–104, 105; policy implementation and, 23, 24, 25–26, 39, 106–107; public

school, xxi; Purple school, 90, 91, 93, 94, 97, 98, 99, 100; Q-Comp and, 24, 29, 33, 39; recruiting, xxi; Red school, 90, 91–92, 94, 97–98, 100; role of, 9, 81, 83; school improvement and, 39; school success and, 81, 82; sensemaking and, 33–34, 38, 39; socialization process, 83, 85, 91, 95, 98, 100, 105, 108; succession, xxi, 82, 83–84, 85, 86, 90–91, 98, 100, 101, 105, 108; teacher evaluation and, 3, 11, 12, 41, 42, 43, 44–45, 46–48, 50–51, 57–58, 59–60, 65, 104–105; Teacher Incentive Fund and, 62, 63, 64, 65, 67, 68, 70, 70–72; teacher leadership and, 24; training programs, 83, 105, 107; turnover, xx; White school, 89, 93–94, 95–96, 98, 99

Principal Candidate School, 92, 94–95, 98, 99, 100

professional learning communities (PLCs), 30, 34

Professional Standards for Educational Leaders, 109

public schools, xvii; performance bonuses and, 64; principals, xxi

Purple charter school, 86, 88, 89, 90, 91, 93, 94, 97, 98, 99

Quality Compensation Policy (Q-Comp), viii, xii, 23, 25, 26; Diego Rivera Academy and, 34–37; funding, 33, 36, 37; implementing, 30–31; Lake Charter School and, 29–31; teacher development/leadership and, 24, 26, 27, 30–31, 37; value of, 35

Race to the Top initiative, 41
Red charter school, 86, 88–89, 90, 91–92, 94–95, 97–98, 99
reform, charter school, xvii
research methods: limited, 108; qualitative, 103
role-based leadership, 93
roundtable, Red school, 92, 95
rubric observation, 11, 12, 31, 34, 37, 38, 44
Ryan, Ms., 6, 11, 12, 14, 15, 17, 18, 19

school board, 8, 23, 105
School Improvement Grant (SIG), 29
sensemaking process, 23, 24, 25, 26, 38; principal's, 33–34, 38, 39; teacher's, 23, 24, 32, 33, 36–37, 38, 39, 40
Sherman, Mr., 47, 48, 49–50, 52–53, 55–56, 57
Smith, Ms., 5–7, 9–10, 11, 12–13, 16, 17
special education students, 30
socialization, 88, 97; collective, 95; dimensions of, 84; divestiture, 96; fixed, 90; framework, 84; investiture, 96; principal, 83, 85, 91, 95, 98, 100, 105, 108; organizational, 82; variable, 90
stand-alone charter schools, 23, 82, 106, 107–108; performance management systems and, 61, 62, 66, 76–78
standardized student achievement test scores, 61
Star Academy, 5, 6, 19. *See also* Ryan, Ms.
start-up charter school, 85
state accountability/standards, xviii, 1, 2, 104, 106; autonomy and, 17–20
student achievement, xvii, 20, 22, 27, 41, 49, 61, 63, 68, 77, 81, 82, 85, 89, 97
student performance, xviii
students: African American, 5, 50, 88–89; American Indian, 30; Asian, 30; Asian American, 30, 88; English learner, 30; Hispanic, 30; Latino, 88–89; low-income, 61, 63; recruiting, 2; special education, 30
succession, ix, 88; planned continuity and, 84; principal, xxi, 82, 83–84, 85, 86, 90–91, 98, 100, 101, 105, 108; unplanned continuity and, 84
summative evaluation of teaching (SET), 63–64, 67, 70, 72–76

Teacher Advancement Program, 26
teacher: advancement, 26; bonuses/pay-for-performance, 31, 61, 63, 64, 65, 70, 71, 72, 74, 77, 78; career opportunities, 24, 26; characteristics, xix; charter school, xviii; compensation, 10, 11; Danielson Framework and, 48, 49, 50, 64; development, 20, 21; evaluation, xii, xx, 24, 26, 64–65, 77, 78; hiring, 3,

10; leadership, xii, 23, 24, 26–27, 28, 30–31, 32, 34, 35–36, 40, 88, 92–95, 96, 99, 100, 104–105; mentoring, 27, 35, 52, 53–54; non-tenured, 62; non-union, 62; pay/salary, 24, 26, 36, 37, 62, 69; performance, 12; performance management systems and, 61; policy implementation and, 26; professional development, 24; Q-Comp and, 24, 25, 26–27, 28, 29–32, 34–37, 39; retaining, 43, 44, 55–56, 57, 59, 63; salary, 24, 26, 36, 37, 62, 69; sensemaking and, 23, 24, 32, 36–37, 38, 39, 40; Teacher Incentive Fund and, 61, 62–63, 68–69, 70; tenure, 62; Three Pillars and, 29, 33, 38; turnover, xix, xix–xx, 10, 16. *See also* teacher evaluation policies

teacher evaluation policies, 41; credibility, 51; data analysis, 50–51; data collection, 47–48, 51; limitations, 51; mentors and, 52, 53–54, 57, 60; Michigan and, 43, 46; Ms. Cohen and, 47, 48, 49, 52, 53–54, 57; Mr. Sherman and, 47, 48, 49; new teacher and, 41; principals and, 41–42, 43–45, 46–48, 50–51, 57–58, 59–60, 65, 104–105; public schools and, 42, 44; standardized, 42; teacher retention and, 55–56, 57, 59, 60

Teacher's Incentive Fund (TIF), xii, 61, 62–64, 65, 67, 68–69, 70, 74, 75, 76, 77

Three Pillars framework, 29, 33, 38

transportation, 14

turnover: principal, xx; teacher, xix, xix–xx, 10, 16

unions, 62, 64

University of California, Berkeley Teacher Incentive Fund and, 63

video, performance management and, 63, 69, 78

West Hawaii Exploration Academy, viii

West, Mr., 6, 9, 10, 11, 12, 14, 15, 17, 18, 19

White charter school, 86, 88, 89, 93–94, 98, 99

About the Editors

Marytza A. Gawlik is an assistant professor in the Educational Leadership and Policy Studies Department at Florida State University. Her research examines various aspects of charter schools including leadership, accountability, autonomy, succession and socialization. Dr. Gawlik has authored several research articles related to charter school leadership and policy.

Dana L. Bickmore is an associate professor in the Educational Policy and Leadership program at the University of Nevada, Las Vegas. Her research explores principal leadership in middle and charter schools. Her work is informed by her 28 years in public education as a teacher, principal, and district administrator. Dr. Bickmore has authored numerous research articles examining school principal leadership.

www.ingramcontent.com/pod-product-compliance
Lightning Source LLC
Chambersburg PA
CBHW021851300426
44115CB00005B/119